Pilgrim Among the Shadows

BORIS PAHOR

Pilgrim Among the Shadows

TRANSLATED FROM THE SLOVENE
BY MICHAEL BIGGINS

A HELEN AND KURT WOLFF BOOK

HARCOURT BRACE & COMPANY

New York   San Diego   London

First published 1967 by Zalozba Obzorja Maribor
English translation copyright © 1995 by Harcourt Brace & Company

Requests for permission to make copies of any part
of the work should be mailed to:
Permissions Department, Harcourt Brace & Company,
6277 Sea Harbor Drive, Orlando,
Florida 32887-6777.

This is a translation of *Nekropola*.

Library of Congress Cataloging-in-Publication Data
Pahor, Boris.
[Nekropola. English]
Pilgrim among the shadows/Boris Pahor; translated from the
Slovene by Michael Biggins.—1st ed.
p.   cm.
"A Helen and Kurt Wolff book."
ISBN 0-15-171958-6
1. Pahor, Boris. 2. World War, 1939–1945—Prisoners and prisons,
German. 3. World War, 1939–1945—Personal narratives, Slovenian.
4. Holocaust, Jewish (1939–1945)—Personal narratives, Slovenian.
5. World War, 1939–1945—Medical care. 6. Political prisoners—
Slovenia—Biography. 7. Physicians—Slovenia—Biography.
8. Slovenia—History—1918–1945.   I. Biggins, Michael.   II. Title.
D805.G3P2613   1995
940.53'18'092—dc20   94-20605

Designed by Lori J. McThomas
Printed in the United States of America
First edition
A B C D E

Cold ashes lie over the shadows.

—SREČKO KOSOVEL

Pilgrim Among the Shadows

It's a Sunday afternoon, and the smooth and sinuous asphalt strip that leads ever higher into the mountains is not as desolate as I would have wished it to be. Cars pass me or return down into the valley, toward Schirmeck, and the volume of tourist traffic disrupts, defiles, even, the calm I had anticipated. Admittedly, my car and I are now a part of the motorized procession. I had hoped that if there was no other traffic but me, my former intimacy with this place would keep my intrusion from distorting the dreamlike images that have lived untouched in the shadows of my mind ever since the war. I realize that some vague resistance is forming in me—resistance to the fact that this mountainous region, such an integral part of our inner world, should be laid bare, made accessible. My resistance is tinged with jealousy, because these outsiders are coming to sightsee in the place that witnessed our anonymous captivity. But—and I sense this unmistakably—their eyes will never see the abyss of desolation that was our punishment for believing in man's dignity and freedom. At the same time I feel an unbidden and gently persistent satisfaction that this mountain in the Vosges is no

longer the site of a distant, self-consuming fury of destruction;
that it has become, instead, the destination of endless crowds
which, naïve and guileless though they may be, are sincere
in their wish to experience just a hint of the inconceivable
fate of their lost brothers.

Maybe in the ascent here there is something of the fervor
of religious pilgrimages to the remote peaks of holy mountains. But nothing in this pilgrimage is even remotely connected to the blind idolatry that Primus Truber so fervently
opposed when he exhorted the Slovenes to discover their
own inner enlightenment and not spend themselves in superficial, pompous ritual. People all over Europe are coming
together on high mountain terraces where human evil wrung
victory after victory out of human pain and nearly set the
seal of permanence on destruction. It isn't the search for
miracle that brings these modern pilgrims. They come here
to tread on truly holy ground, to pay homage to the ashes
of fellow creatures who by their mute presence have raised,
in our hearts, an immovable landmark of human history.

On the sharp turns I probably do not think of the rocking
of the truck as it brought back a box from Markirch con-
taining our first corpse. At the time I didn't even know I
was sitting on such sad cargo. But the frigid air would have
paralyzed any thought before it could form. No, I most certainly do not think of any of the images that persist in me,
tangled and crowded like a withered and moldy bunch of

grapes. Through my windshield I watch the strip of smooth asphalt before me and would rather it be some old, buckling, pothole-ridden road leading into the more authentic world of the past. But I can't deny being spoiled and selfish like any other modern driver accustomed to the comfort of a smooth ride at high speed. I try to visualize a mountain highway in Slovenia comparable to this serpentine road from Schirmeck to Struthof. I picture the switchbacks leading to Vršič—but there the road opens onto a panorama of rocky peaks which is lacking here. The road from Kobarid to Drež-nica? That could almost be a match. But then again, not really, because there is no Krn here, with its blinding cliffs. Maybe this road through the Vosges is most like the winding road that rises up out of Kobarid to Vršno. There the forest also gives way now and then to scenic views of the valley below, which never seems that far away. And there are no cliffs, just a constant alternation of dense forest and rolling grassy field. I can't remember whether the pines on the slopes of Vršno are the same as here. Probably not.

The road still leads uphill, although here and there accompanied by the whiteness of hewn rock, as in any place where human implements have wounded the earth's green flanks and dug into its accumulated, hidden wealth.

To the left, a long, wide stretch of open ground appears, and it leads to the entrance. Some day this stretch will be lined with trees. Now it's jammed with buses and cars symmetrically arrayed from one end to the other, so that I can't help thinking of the huge parking lot outside the caves at Postojna. As best as I can, I resist the image of aging Swiss and Austrian tourists. Gray-haired wives possessively clutch the straps of their old-fashioned purses and rotate their heads in the direction of the tour guide's voice, like chickens startled from their little tasks. The most honest thing I could do now would be to drive away and return tomorrow morning, when the more humdrum atmosphere of the work week can be expected to have a less jarring effect on these isolated, step-like terraces. But tomorrow other landscapes have been mapped out for me, and I walk toward the entrance, conscious that I am depending mechanically on my quick and hectic schedule instead of taking in the surroundings first. I feel a gentle nostalgia for that undisturbed, timeless composure in which a person can relate himself honestly to the earth and sea, to streets and houses, to the faces and lives that fate brings him in contact with. But impatience drives us feverishly on, and we receive only superficial impressions, which disperse like water spraying from the prow of a motorboat. In the end we take comfort in our nostalgia for permanence, as though the awareness of that disfiguring loss was itself a kind of wealth. Which perhaps it is. And may always have been, although today we are actually impoverished by the abundance of experiences. We've done the precise opposite of what bees do. Scattering pollen over a million objects, we persist in hoping—despite the quiet voice that tells us it's impossible—that someday we will have the time to replenish our abandoned hive.

It's absurd, but I almost feel that the tourists walking back to their cars can see the striped jacket wrapped around my shoulders and hear my wooden clogs crunch on the gravel of the path. This is a sudden flash, the kind that confuses past and present. There are moments when an invisible but powerful force stirs within us; others can sense it—as the presence of something unusual in the air—and they shudder like a boat in an unexpected wave. I may well be showing something of my former self. At this thought I try to focus on my stride. It bothers me that my sandals are so light and my step so elastic, more than if I were wearing canvas shoes with thick wooden soles. As I did then.

The door, strung with barbed wire, is closed, just as it used to be. Nothing has changed. Only the guards are missing in the towers. You still have to wait at the door. The only difference is that now a watchman emerges from a wooden hut, unlocks the door, and at carefully measured intervals allows groups into his pitiless mountain corral. Thanks to this procedure calm reigns on the camp's descending terraces. The July sun steadfastly keeps watch over the silence, and only occasionally, somewhere far below, the words of a tour guide echo like the halting voice of some evangelist risen from the dead.

The watchman recognizes me, which is surprising; I didn't think he would remember my visit last year. "*Ça va?*" he asks. It is just enough to strike a note of intimacy, separating me from the swarm of tourists. He's dark-haired and plain, short and sinewy and animated. If he had a helmet and lantern, he'd make a perfect miner. But he's intelligent, too. It's obvious that he is embarrassed, feels uncomfortable with me, a former inmate. After all, he earns his living by conducting tours through the land of our death. So I take the ready permission that he gives me to proceed alone into the region of barbed wire not just as a sign of his comradely regard but as his way of getting rid of me promptly. More the latter. Nor do I resent it, knowing that I myself could never speak to a fellow visitor, even one who had been with me in the place of crematoria. I would be afraid of slipping into cliché at every word. It's impossible, anyway, to talk about death—or love—with anyone but yourself. Death and love allow no witnesses.

When he speaks to the silent crowd as their tour guide, he is in fact speaking to his memories, a monologue of self-revelation. It isn't clear whether this release satisfies or calms him to any degree. I imagine he feels even more ill at ease after such testimony—certainly lessened. But I am grateful to him for letting me walk through this inaudible world alone. I feel superior, satisfied with the special privilege that comes from my former status as an outcast. Now as then, separateness and silence. For despite the crowds and our herdlike existence, each of us lived in isolation, in his own mute darkness.

I am incapable of measuring the distance between myself and the steps, familiar and close as they are in the sunlight; I sense only the pall of nothingness that hangs over them. They are simple, as the emaciated arms were simple that carried and set the stones they are made of. They once seemed steeper to me. The adult returns to the land of his childhood, only to discover how small the buildings of his memory really are, forgetting that he measured the world from Tom Thumb's perspective. But it wasn't in our childhood that we went up and down these stairs; our helplessness was greater than a child's, for we lacked the advantage of innocence. Each of us, in his nakedness, in his withered skin of a hungry animal burning itself out in captivity, each day calculated the distance between the ovens and his emaciated rib cage, his sticklike arms and legs. I could use Carlo Collodi's wooden boy as a metaphor, since Pinocchio, too, was fated to be seared by flame. But his gentle creator replaced the damaged parts, which no one ever thought of doing for us. No, Pinocchio is inappropriate here, yet some day we must find a contemporary Collodi to tell children the story of our past. The question is, will he be able to impress a child's heart without injuring it with the evil, and guard it also from the temptations of the future? On these steps, which bend at each terrace like great stone knees, we reverted to a pre-rational state. This happened as the cytoplasm in our cells and the marrow in our bones dried up, like a jellyfish on gravel. Then the steps loomed before us like a flight of stairs in a belltower. There seemed to be no end to the succession of terraces. Another reason it took us an eternity to reach the top was that our feet, though our legs were like sticks, had swollen into white, fleshy lumps.

Time, I've realized, is my accomplice, and I stop to look out over the tall grass beyond the wire fence. I let myself be transported back to the yellowed commons in the Karst village I walked through just the other day. By comparison, this long, sparse mane of hay is pathetic in its endurance. Its vegetable persistence is senseless. This grass was here before *it,* it was here the entire time that *it* lasted, and now it is here and just the same. Its withered and faded yellow frailty—the existence of any grass, of all the grasses in the world—becomes absurd. Earth's plants and creatures offer man no intimacy; they stand mute beside him, caught in the imperative to grow. Blossoms flaring atop stems, for all their variety and vivid color, are essentially blind. Amid such thoughts, I am glad I am alone and that the tour group with its guide has moved beyond the terraces, leaving the entrance far above remote and concealed. Jealous of my solitude, I salvage the monotony of my own memories, but at the same time am bitterly aware that the crowd of people with its slow, uniform movements mirrors, more often than not, the heartless existence, albeit in a different dimension, of all those blasted, faded blades of grass.

I just saw Tolya coming down the steps in front of me, grumbling because an emaciated corpse had slid forward in the canvas groove of the stretcher we were carrying, its shaved head bumping him in the small of his back. I was glad the corpse hadn't touched me, and clumsily regained my footing, hiking the handles up on my end so they wouldn't hit my knees. I didn't mind picking up a naked, mummified body from its straw tick and putting it onto the stretcher's crude, spotted canvas, I did that work naturally and with ease, but I hated it when a body we were carrying downhill touched me of its own accord. Perhaps living cells don't object to touching dead cells if the contact is intended, the result of their own activity, their own centrifugal, living choice; but they cannot bear the non-willed intrusion from outside, of dead tissue on warm, elastic living. This rule isn't limited to the camps; it applies in daily life.

I wonder what images the visitors will conjure for themselves as they gather around the tour guide. Photographs enlarged to enormous proportions, hung in the barracks, showing a multitude of shaved heads, jutting cheekbones, and keyhole-shaped jaws, may raise on the movie screen of their minds a vague semblance of our reality then. But no screen could ever show the state of a man convinced that his neighbor just got a half finger more yellow liquid in his tin cup than he did. You might be able to approximate the fierce look in the eyes that only hunger gives, but it is impossible to reproduce the urgency of the mouth's mucous membranes or the contractions of the esophagus. How could any picture capture the endless subtleties of that unseen battle in which all the precepts of civilization collapse under the tyranny of the stomach lining? I don't know which gland predominates, or which lining, the esophagus, the stomach. But I do know that my dog Žužko, of whom I'm normally quite fond, becomes unbearable when the saliva starts running in his muzzle and he anxiously swallows it, fidgeting impatiently with his forepaws. When I look him in the eyes then, I see we are related, the main difference between us being that he sits on his haunches while I sit on the latest product of a Karst furniture factory.

The celluloid of a movie camera could certainly capture the early-morning shoving of striped uniforms in their cramped beehive as they jump down from their three-tiered bunks and jockey for position in the washroom, each hoping to stake claim to a pair of clogs with the canvas intact so they won't come off that day in the snow, mud, or deep puddles. And film could capture the firm hand shoving the bowling-ball head of a walking skeleton under a stream of water, the rib cage creaking like a dried-out wicker basket as the hand pushes the spine down even more firmly. Outside is the cold and darkness of morning. The barracks door is like a narrow opening to a black abyss, and any second now they'll have to run through it. Or film could show the many-headed assembly at noon, teeming in its collective instinct, shifting back and forth with a shudder of strength generated by the anticipation of a ladleful of some watery but warm energy source. Or this moment: the shaved heads all bent over their wooden spoons. Or the zebra-striped anthill as it prepares to turn in at night, tying its rags in bundles before it can run into that freezer full of ticks. But not before each one steps up on a stool so a man holding a caged light can examine his crotch. There is no pubic hair—the barber's razor has seen to that—but on the ends of the emerging new hairs there might be a few nits. It's as though each penis is illuminated for some new rite of adoration amid a swarm of bodies with shirts to navels and hairless heads like newborn babies. But in this pathetic illumination of crotches there is nothing of the reverence that once chiseled fertility symbols over the doors of Pompeii. It is simply a ritual by which those in power confront their fear of lice and typhus. So the light overtakes the sparrow in its nest, dead from starvation before it could fledge, dangling lifelessly in the inspector's hand. A movie camera could capture such sequences faithfully—dwelling on the long electric cord, moving down it toward the lightbulb and shriveled crotch, catching along the way the shaved heads of men jostling for position so that they can be first to run off to their chilly crypt for the night. Maybe it's just as well there was no camera; for who knows what people today might think of that herd of half-naked creatures taking turns stepping up on the stool while the rest look on fearfully, incredulous that this member, floodlit, exposed, and withered, is the begetter of all the countless specimens of their two-legged breed. A good thing there was no film—today these wizened creatures with their crotches on display could be taken for a pack of trained dogs, taught through hunger to stand on a stool on their hind legs and sniff each other's parts.

It was worse when the block fell under quarantine for typhus—no distant phantom, but an everyday reality. At those times there was no morning or noon or evening fall-in for roll call, no endless standing about in the morning after columns from the other terraces had left for the quarry. Inactivity then wasn't graced even with the movement that gave us the impression of some variation amid our slow wasting away. For while our clockwork comings and goings were only the languid shifting of a dead sea, their rhythmic motion gave some dim sense of purpose. Confinement to the barracks deprived us of even that illusion. Even the barbed wire and its electric current receded into the distance then, and the barracks became the wooden hut of lepers on an island from which the last human boat has stolen away forever.

Bizarre as it may seem, it is a fact that the little finger of my left hand made it possible for me to stand here now and relive this past. Shortly before one quarantine, Bogaerts, a Belgian surgeon, made three incisions in my palm to drain some stubborn pus, and the watery blood that welled up gave sad witness to what remained of the resistance of the organism through which it circulated. If the wound refused to heal—which was a bad sign—the white bandage at least served to protect me from the vigilant eyes that came looking for able-bodied serial numbers. For that reason I kept the paper bandage on long after I could have discarded it; it was like a precious possession that is all the more precious the more fragile it becomes. I cradled an infant that at first had a white, round head, which gradually shrank and turned gray, until finally it took on the appearance of a callused and grimy fist. Even as such it was an extraordinary talisman that faithfully repelled unwanted attention. I doubt that anyone ever worked so hard and long to preserve a crepe-paper bandage, that anyone ever tended so a tissue as delicate as froth and becoming more tattered each day. Later, quarantine delivered us from fear of the transports, at least for a while. Even then I clung to my concern for the bandaged pustule. At the end of our isolation period there would be new selections for the work detachments. And what about typhus? Certainly the danger was always lurking, though no one seemed to think of it as a mortal enemy. Perhaps each of us had the subconscious hope that the disease would pass and not touch him. As long as you were untouched, typhus remained invisible, absent. But we all knew what the members of work details looked like when they were brought back to camp. Their feet were wrapped in strips of paper from cement bags and cinched with wire. The medics would unwrap them to discover gaping, festering lesions which were long and wide in the middle and pointed at both ends, resembling yellowed palm fronds. The majority couldn't get down from the trucks themselves. When they were put on the ground, they would squat or lie until someone finally hauled them off to the showers. Three-foot-long tongs, clamped around the neck, were used on those who had stopped breathing. (Someone would do well to study the psychological make-up of the person who designed those tongs, which made it possible to move a body onto a heap of other bodies and then to the iron lift beneath the ovens.)

One day Jean, a French doctor, visited our block to re-bandage wounds. He smiled when he saw my hand, yet put a new strip of paper on it and let me keep playing hide-and-seek with my fate. Our acquaintance might have ended with that had Jean been just a conscientious physician and not a sympathetic fellow prisoner as well. The Slovene talent for learning foreign languages also helped me. I can't say whether that ability of ours is a sign of psychological wealth, of an active and multifaceted mind, or whether it simply is an elasticity that we've acquired over the centuries through in-cessant bowing, scraping, and accommodating. In this re-spect we resemble the Jews and Gypsies. But also like those two tribes, ours has resisted assimilation throughout its history.

Jean was in high spirits, even though the crowd jostled us, making the barracks resemble the inside of a Gypsy wagon in motion. He asked how it was I was not an Italian when I wore a red triangle with a capital I in the middle. He bandaged my hand and listened as I explained the end of the First World War to him, the Treaty of London, and the Slovene littoral. So that means you speak Slovene at home, he said. That's right. And that means, he continued, that you can understand a Czech, or a Pole, or a Russian? I smiled, as though Jean had discovered something I had been unaware of until that moment. For what had become of those distant days when young Croatians from Istria taught me their melodious language? The African sands had since shifted for me, too, and two years interpreting for Yugoslav prisoners of war on Lake Garda had almost been obliterated from memory. I would never have thought that those experiences could help me in my battle with death. Jean (I didn't know his name yet) was pleased that I knew French, and he wrapped the bandage slowly while I told him that I had taken two courses in Padua on French literature, the first one on Baudelaire's *Fleurs du mal,* and the second one a year later on his *Poèmes en prose.* We were now wedged into the thick of the zebra-striped mass of people, so our conversation became like a hurried confession, or the dictation of a last will and testament when every second counts. Jean was particularly interested in my German. I learned that Leif, a Norwegian doctor who was head of the clinic, which was simply a barracks for sick prisoners, knew only English and German after his native language. Everything official had to be written in German—whatever concerned the patients, disease, or death. Jean asked if I knew how to write German, and it dawned on me that he had passed from friendly interest in a new French-speaking acquaintance to business matters. I felt an internal flutter, like a bud opening in spring. I doubt that I thought at that moment of our German teacher, Herr Kitter, who had made a difficult life in Koper even worse with the failing grades he wrote at the bottom of my German assignments. I am sure I could have mastered German, if I hadn't been so resistant. Every fiber of my being was opposed to it. "Of course I can write German," I said, "especially if it means working with people who are trying to save us from the ovens."

The next day I forgot about Jean; the phantom of him vanished as quickly as it had appeared, like a bubble rising through mud to the green of a lone germinating shoot, then popping. I also couldn't believe that the young Frenchman was already a doctor; he was probably still only a medical student trying to save himself from destruction with an innocent lie. We were all so intimate with destruction that we moved through it like sleepwalkers. And just as one should never rouse a sleepwalker when he is balanced over an abyss, so we knew to resist temptation in those rare moments when an image from the real world stirred inside us. Lest we lose our balance altogether.

And so for a week I thought and felt nothing amid the crush of humanity locked up for typhus, a mass amorphously shifting in the barracks as though in a nailed crate, until I heard a long, familiar number called out in German. All illusions had been purged from our minds when we were still quite young, and we were taught to expect only evil, evil thorough and apocalyptic. The child who was once caught in the panic of a crowd as he helplessly watched flames destroy a theater in the center of Trieste had his vision of the future ruined forever. The blood-red sky above the harbor, the wild fascists who dumped gasoline on the proud building and then danced around its furious pyre—all this impressed itself on the child's mind, traumatizing it. And this was only the beginning, because later the boy became a criminal, without knowing against whom or what he had transgressed; he did not understand that he had been condemned for using the language in which he expressed his love for his parents and with which he first came to know the world. In the process of punishment, the authorities began changing the first and last names of thousands upon thousands of Slovenes—and not just the living, but also the populations of whole cemeteries. This annulment, lasting a quarter of a century, reached its ultimate degree in the camps, when the individual was reduced from a name to a number. But now, despite the countless shifting gray-and-blue picket fences of our uniforms, the string of German syllables in the inarticulate air was directed only at me. It was as though someone had dropped a lifeline into the depths of me. I was elated at the sudden discovery that I could be useful to this doomed group and thus deliver myself from anonymous death. At the same time I was sober, calm, equanimous, not really expecting that the rope would be long enough to reach the bottom where I sat. This was no virtue, merely an instinct acquired from the long certainty that the powers of destruction held an infinite advantage over any microscopic organism trying to hold on to its faith in survival.

To this day I carry a permanent memento of that morning in quarantine, because my little finger in its paper dressing slowly bent, as though trying to cling to the bandage that would save it. It remains bent at a ninety-degree angle, reminding me of itself over and over. At first it teased me. When I washed, it would get caught in an ear or nostril. If that happened, instead of getting angry I would greet it like an old friend, an entity separate from myself. Later, when I became reacclimated to daily life, the hooked finger began to bother me—as when, for instance, a girlfriend took me by the hand, or when I would gesture in my classroom and all the students focused on the jutting digit. At such moments I was almost ashamed of it. The sight of that little deformity brought to mind a villain in a pre-war movie, his mutilated hand replaced by a sharply pointed iron hook. In some bizarre way I began to identify myself with that bent implement at the end of the villain's arm, and with the tongs that the stokers used to haul our corpses by the neck. Several times I have been on the verge of asking a surgeon friend of mine to do something about my finger, but always stopped at the thought that a hook may also save a climber from doom on a sheer rock face.

The steps again. Somewhere close by was Block 6, which in the early days bore the sign WEBEREI. Subsequently all the buildings on this side became part of the infirmary. *Weberei,* weaving mill. What strange weavers we were. Granted, it was impossible to exact better work from such a debilitated group, but that word for the pathetic job we did could only have been used in a place where all values fell before the black derision of the ovens. Heaps of rubber and canvas strips were piled up on the tables before us like the bundles of colorful rummage a ragman hordes in his stall. Our job was to slice these scraps into thin bands by pushing them against small, sharp blades set into the wooden surface of the tables, and then twist them into colorful braids. Someone would use these to make the thick pads that protected the sides of ships from being scraped by stone piers. But hunger wove a gray gauze over our eyes, and we couldn't see such ships. We hunched over the noodle-like tatters as if over a nest of snakes linked to each other and twisting and reshaping themselves in the gloom. With our weakness and sitting in one place so long, it would have been easy to nod off, but twitching exhaustion kept us awake and forced our heavy eyelids back open. The pre-dawn cold retreated into the forgotten past, and beyond the windowpanes the morning light promised that the Atlantic wind would assault our striped sackcloth less harshly. This was the hour when our self-satisfied young Kapo would slice a rectangular loaf of bread—our rations—and start looking around at the multitude of seated stripes. Who can say, maybe the deliberateness of his slicing was intended to quicken the activity of the stomachs waiting. Or maybe he was childishly enjoying his self-importance, his power to choose favorites and receive their gratitude. None of the shaved heads are sure whether they should lift and straighten to be more visible, to be noticed, or instead bend even more conscientiously over the blades, in the quiet, desperate hope that their diligence in the face of temptation will be rewarded. There are eyes conscious of having fallen shut just as the Kapo looked in their direction; they watch the thin slices of bread, these eyes above attenuated noses, eyes gleaming with the gray rapacity of birds of prey, and in the next moment humiliated, pleading. And there are eyes that were on the verge of pleading but held back at the last moment, lowering to watch their fingers scrabble mindlessly over the rough boards.

This is where I found myself seated next to Gabriele one morning, once we had jostled our way into the barracks after a long and frigid roll call. His head was big and round, and his body just as round, totally unlike the bodies of the invalids and convalescents assigned to the *Weberei*. But that wasn't surprising; the steady flow of new transports accustomed us to the fact that there would always be some robust bodies. No, it wasn't his roundess that caught my attention, it was the gestures and movements, the familiar half-questioning, half-anxious way his head turned toward me. Even before he had a chance to speak, I knew that I had met someone like him, the same lively eyes behind thick lenses, on a streetcar in Trieste or at noon on the sidewalk near where the Corso meets the Via Romana. There are certain qualities of our countrymen which, although impossible to describe, are so unique that even far from home they evoke the street corner by your house, the old signboard over the neighborhood dairy. It's almost as though our native region has left its mark on our faces, its image wavering on our cheekbones, in our dimples, in the indentation under the nose, like summer heat over asphalt. The words that come from such faces are less astonishing, because you have anticipated them. But they are nevertheless splendid for what they conjure up. The presence of your home town, which has become so tenuous in this place. You feel it like a stare fixed at you from the side—and which you try to avoid, because the first condition for even the slightest chance of survival is to eliminate from your mind any image that does not belong in the kingdom of evil. The result is that even those whom death ultimately pardons feel themselves so saturated with death that despite their new freedom they remain inextricably bound to it. This is why my conversations with Gabriele, full of uncertainty over how much longer we would retain our sedentary, even life-restoring jobs, never wandered far from the ovens. His bewildered expression seemed to beg for words of assurance from me, since I had already been assigned to work details outside the camp and was experienced and fully initiated in his eyes. It was also the expression of a lost and isolated human being who believed that I had a multitude of fellow Slovene prisoners by my side, and that my tribal allegiance could provide him with some security. Here, where we had long ago passed life's border stone, we Slovenes were no longer separated by citizenship. More than language brought us together now; in our resistance against the exterminator of our kind we had become united in suffering and the search for some common salvation.

Gabriele spoke of democracy and coexistence on our shared littoral, and his eyes darted from me to the long cloth strips on the table, then back to me, as though afraid I did not believe these new words. And true, as I listened, they did seem strange to me, though professions of brotherhood indeed could have been prompted by our abnormal surroundings. Amid the ultimate equality of hunger and ashes it becomes impossible to hold on to class distinctions. I was struck by the irony that after so many years of living on the same streets and the same coastline, a fellow citizen, a member of the Italian elite, should address me in human terms for the first time here, where everything human had been put into question. And though clearly the undeniable equality of our condemned bodies had removed every obstacle, I still balked at the thought of our shared fear of the ovens playing godfather at the baptism of this new brotherhood.

Fear had been the air our community breathed from the end of the First World War, since the days the books were swept off the shelves of our libraries and burned beneath the monument to Verdi, to the delight of the Italians. And fear became our daily bread when our local theaters were razed, or when a fascist shot at a Slovene preacher in a church by the Canale, or when a consumptive village schoolmaster spat in the face of a young girl who had dared to speak in her native tongue. After so much history, didn't these noble overtures now in the land of crematoria come too late? Would an Italian from Trieste call you brother if he too was not being threatened with destruction? But I didn't argue with him. I was glad that he had said the words, but immediately set them aside, as though consigning them to the life that flowed infinitely far away from these grim steps. Later, when we again sat next to each other, we made no mention of Trieste, but spoke in a kindred way of hunger, and watched in silence as the thin slices of bread made false starts in our direction. Possibly at such moments our biological nature took priority over the friendship that derives from a common native land, and our starved cells outshouted all else, so that each of us saw the square sliver of bread moving only toward *him*, since it would have been impossible for the Kapo to reward both of us at once. No, the cells definitely won out. Even if a man gives no outward sign, whether because he's too exhausted, or too stubborn, or too proud, or a fatalist, the animal within silently opens its jaws and bares its claws.

With total clarity I can see Gabriele standing outside his barracks, the one above the crematorium. At that time, thanks to Jean, I was already acting as an interpreter. Gabriele hoped to make contact with his family in Trieste, something that seemed almost realistic after the formation of the new German province of Adriatisches Küstenland. I was skeptical, but gave him the address of Elza Kleč in Maribor and told him she would be able to get his mail to his family, as she had done for me. I don't know if he wrote to her; perhaps that path seemed too circuitous for him. But I did write Elza about him, and she passed the information on to my family, who in turn contacted his. Later Elza managed to send him something, although it was not much; she wasn't wealthy, and still isn't. Maybe he did write her, after all. Camp life eventually separated us; the endless crowd came between us.

I met him only once after that, in Dachau. By then his eyes had stopped their restless wandering. He had finally been broken. He sat on the ground next to one of the barracks to the right of the main avenue. He was exhausted but still in command of himself. His shirt front was open; it was autumn, but not yet cold. His expression was calmer, but also more vacant. I don't remember for whom he was waiting, if anyone, or where he was headed, if anywhere. That was in the days after they evacuated us from here, when we slept in paper sleeping bags that rustled all night long. Then we were locked up in quarantine, which a few were able to leave, taken to Munich to clear rubble after an air attack. Gabriele wanders through my memory like a lost soul, the image of the lone traveler who steps out of an endless row of zebra stripes and sits down for a while to rest on his long journey to eternity.

I've reached the bottom now.

Two barracks here have been left untouched, as have two barracks up at the top, near the entrance. One was for solitary confinement. The silence of its open doorway is like the silence that hung over this barracks as we moved about the upper terraces, feeling its presence but averting our eyes from it, just as we averted our thoughts from the ovens that blazed incessantly in the building next to it. And now, as I face the open cells, and see the wooden horse on which the victim was stretched out, naked to the waist, in preparation for the lashes that would flay his back, I cannot empathize with him or even pity him. It is as though I'm transfixed by the silence that has gripped all the prisoners on the terraces. Someone has snuck off to rest somewhere, has lain down, and his eyes are slowly closing. Infuriated men search the wooden bunks and latrines, and the heavy silence is broken only by the barking of a German shepherd irritated by the tension in the air. As we stood in our close rows on the narrow ledges that evening, none of us pictured the wooden horse that now bears the printed sign: CHEVALET À LA BASTONNADE. That is, we didn't think of the punishment in store for the poor devil so much as we held our breath for the moment when he would sit up suddenly at the unexpected thunder of jack-boots and find himself alone in the barracks, and then alone before the silent rows stretching skyward like a striped pyramid. We were terrified by his separation from our tight ranks, which the silence and the alarm had made even tighter. There was also an instinctive repudiation of him in the way we followed his progress. The dull awareness that they had taken him to one of the cells, and that the SS boots would finally stop echoing up and down the stairs to the right and left of us, brought us relief. The hunger and beatings he would suffer didn't concern us. What concerned us was his loneliness there, next to the building with the ovens, his solitary confinement on this lowermost terrace.

On the other side of the barbed wire here are pine trees. But now as then, it seems to me that I am not standing near a forest. I can't help seeing these trunks as lifeless objects, stage scenery to accompany this fenced-in excavation. Not once in the entire time I was here did I consider the forest a part of nature. I recall destroying it in my thoughts, burning it the night they brought the Alsatians to the camp and herded them into the cell block. There were several men and even one priest in the group, but the rest, about a hundred, were young women. They must have known about the boneyard here, a thousand meters up in their own mountains. Though not many saw it, they were aware that it existed, that it was built on several terraces, and that the chimney on the lowest terrace was continually belching smoke. They also had heard the German shepherds barking on the hillside. So the women surely sensed what was in store when the trucks proceeded slowly up the steep switchbacks. They may have held on to hope, because the Allies were in Belfort now, and they probably thought some help might come from the Alsatian resistance. But deep down, where one is seldom mistaken, they knew the truth. Just as we did, watching from our quiet barracks the arrival of the trucks. We sensed that this signalled change. The realization that our overlords were retreating and had no idea what to do with their prisoners was a spark of light in eyes that had grown used to the dark. We became restless, though our new uneasiness focused on the barracks as it belched fire and smoke into the mountain sky, a gray locomotive without wheels, with a fiery corona hovering over its chimney like the flame atop the smokestack of some renegade refinery. We had grown accustomed to the chimney and the stench saturating the air, and so could view the newcomers with a certain superiority. Yet the pathetic sense of special status our intimacy with destruction gave us only heightened the futility of our resistance to the death of these living, resilient, yet delicate bodies. A dumb tension rose from our powerlessness, only to dissipate into powerlessness: our manhood, suddenly awakened, confronted the annihilation of a woman's body, joining Eros and death in an unspeakably cruel way. For we were males trapped in shriveled bodies, but we had also just become aroused lovers sentenced at the moment of our arousal to eternal solitude. The absurdity of existence mingled with our stillborn manhood beneath the chimney with its blood-red tulip at the top. At the same time our minds shied from too clear a recognition of that absurdity, as one withdraws from a flood.

The fate of those young women's bodies intensified the agonizingly helpless protest in our own drained bodies. We should have stormed out of the barracks, flown down the steps, and attacked the cell block from which SS officers were leading the women one by one, twenty meters across the way, to the ovens. From the guard towers machine guns would have mown down the zebra-striped rabble, and huge searchlights would have blinded us. But we would have redeemed ourselves, delivered ourselves from the humiliation that clung to our innermost being. No such thought crossed the minds of this hungry crowd; protest had been washed away with the dysentery. When skin turns to parchment and thighs are as thick as ankles, then the mind flickers like a dying battery, a barely perceptible, occasional, timid vibration, bubbles rising from a great depth to burst when they reach the surface.

The forest close by was innocent, and yet I reproached it then for not offering in its dense recesses refuge from destruction. Through the forest I condemned all of nature, nature reaching vertically for the sun even after sunlight had lost all meaning. I cursed the trees, because the liberators we had awaited for so long, those who would prevent the sacrifice of the Alsatian women, did not emerge from their darkness. And so I projected into these trees all my powerlessness. Today they stand mute and still before me, as though frozen by the curse.

The group of tourists and tour guide approach, so I cross to the other side. The sun warms as it should in midsummer, and the gravel crunches beneath my sandals, evoking Sunday in the park. Which of course I resist, because it seems wrong that visitors should gather their impressions in such a peaceful, dreamy atmosphere. They should be required to walk along the ledge down below, obscured by a high wall of trees, on days when the terraces are in the grip of gloom, rain, and raging wind. Or on winter days, when snow makes the bones harder, when they lose their balance inside the skidding wooden clogs. The white stairs are even more merciless. But the block leader shrieks furiously, "Move! Move!" as he drives the striped stick figures out of the barracks with his club and they topple over one another. Rainwater splashes your bare ankles, or bare feet if the clogs have got lost. At roll call, the striped material hangs on your back like wet newspaper. But a wet death is less violent and less tyrannical than an icy one, especially if you have to run to the showers in the middle of the night as part of the battle against lice and typhus. Running down stairs doesn't warm the body; it delivers it into the embrace of the mountain wind. And the resonant slapping of wooden clogs on stone makes sharp reports in the taut cold. Here, before this anonymous barracks, the bewildered herd hastily undresses to the sound of barking from the other side of the hill, beyond the barbed wire, wire that haltingly slices the night so that pieces of it fall into the bottomless pit of nothingness. "Move! Move!" the splenetic voice drives us on, and the sounds from over the hill grow more and more enraged, as though the nostrils of a many-headed beast have just picked up the scent, borne by the wind over night's shoulder, of our naked flesh. But the door to the washroom is locked, and the lightbulb above the entrance shows a multitude of bare skulls and ladderlike ribs, while all hands are busy twisting rags into bundles. Emaciated limbs shiver, shift back and forth, and hop to fend off the wind. When the bundles are tied with the string that normally holds up trousers, the stick figures rub their forearms and thighs and hug their shoulders, pressing their chins in tight. But soon they drop their arms and put their hands on their stomach, chest, and again stomach. One squats and hugs his knees, but the harsh wind slaps him in the back, so he stands and tries to cover his back with the backs of his hands. His body twists in the dark like laundry in the hands of a washerwoman, and his bald head winces from the wind. The door is still locked. From the forest an owl calls, as if suddenly summoned by the frightened imagination of a child who has taken grandma's fairy tale too much to heart. The ground is littered with rags, from which white naked bodies arise. Here and there someone bends over, grabs a bundle of rags, clutches it con-vulsively, abdomen scissored to thighs and knees like a goalie catching a soccer ball. But many can't stand up, because with their rags they have removed their last strength. They sit on their bundles. The lightbulb above the entrance etches agitated shadows on callused skin stretched over ribs. On this harp of a human chest the wind's cold fingers play a quiet requiem. Then not German shepherd but human bark-ing assaults the night. "Move! Move!" The door opens, steam surges forth, and with it naked bodies. Now the shouting is unnecessary, because the white, warm cloud draws the scram-bling shadows as strongly as the mountain night drives them forward. They quickly fill the square room where dripping showerheads are fixed to the ceiling. Nothing upsets them. They take the barbers' curses as a hearty welcome. Each barber beckons toward his station and brandishes his razor, its blade glistening in the electric light. The guests are glad to move their bodies through the warmth, sit down in the chairs, and offer their heads to the razors that remove the stubbly growth of hair. Or to stand while the barber crouches at their knees and skillfully navigates his razor through the divided harbor of an emaciated crotch. By turns boisterous or angry, each loud Figaro plucks the scrawny fowl destined to be picked even cleaner when the time comes for the oven. A blade scrapes the sparse recess of an armpit, while another artist dips a big mason's brush into a pot and smears a shaven crotch, causing hands instantly to grab the stinging area and squeeze to extinguish the fire. The bodies hop, trying to release some of the burning through movement. One barber sets an old skeleton down on a footstool, because he can't get at him any other way. "Come on, old fellow," he prods. But the statue sways and is on the verge of tipping over onto the wet cement floor like a bundle of firewood rolling off of a grate. "*Verfluchter*," the barber curses and grabs him by the penis to keep him from falling. They finally lay him flat on the floor next to a score of others. Now streams of water are released from the showerheads, and a thicket of bodies jostles in the warmth, arms scrubbing arms with a hard soap that dissolves into yellow rivulets that course the cement like rainwater colored with clay in a downpour. The body loves the countless warm tongues that lick it, and the memory of the night mountain air vanishes for a while and we forget that beneath the shower room is an oven, and that night and day a stoker heaves human logs into it. Even if the bodies think that soon *they* might be used to heat the water, the pleasure offered by this wet warmth is not lessened. Hurriedly they soap up; their crotches have stopped stinging. But those lying on the floor open and close their mouths to a much slower rhythm, as if drawing up air through the entire length of their stick limbs, which disappear in the steam and stretch out toward infinity. Drops of hot water run off their glassy eyes, off their few remaining teeth. But they too must be cleaned, it is the rule, so the ones who have finished washing start to scrub the scaly skin of those prone, as if scouring a grimy floor or soaping the surface of a dried codfish. Meanwhile bodies standing along the wall dry themselves with white towels, grateful they can still stand. But now they can think of nothing except running, because the door has been thrown open and they must go outside, menacing shouts of "Move! Move!" cutting through the night. At the door your hand grabs trousers, jacket, undershirt, and clogs, so that your body can start the race up the steps. Move, move, a whip snaps across someone's just-washed skin. Only the weakest remain inside, trembling as they try to pull their trousers on. Move, move, and yet you manage to stay in the steamy room a moment longer, prolonging the warm embrace as a few lingering drops fall from the showerheads like the last of your lifeblood. Someone drags an emaciated, lifeless body across the cement floor by its heels. The barbers call raucously to another group, newcomers, and now you have no choice but to run with the herd as it scurries half-naked up the steps, grabbing at stray clogs or picking up lost trousers and tucking them under arm. The block leader's shouts come from far below, because our herd has been scattered over the first, second, and third terraces, some even farther up. On the fourth terrace they will bring their skin into the refuge of the barracks long before the others.

Under the clear, sunny sky these images become implausible, and I realize that our forced processions have moved into the unreal realm of the past forever. They will become shadows in mankind's collective subconscious; they will haunt some with a dim sense of guilt, and possibly drive some to acts of aggression, in that way to rid themselves of pangs of conscience. That is why it would be fitting for tour guides to bring these scenes of past evil to life in the visitors' imagination. No, it is futile. A legion of guides would be needed to awaken all of Europe.

I stand outside the barracks and think how much it looks like a shack where workers asphalting a road or putting up a new building keep their equipment—a metaphor prompted by the clear light of summer. When I was here two years ago and a carpenter who was replacing rotten boards complained what awkward work it was, I had a different reaction. Of course I felt gratified that the French were taking such pains to maintain the wooden monument, but at the same time I didn't like the presence of white new wood among the dark, weathered boards. Not so much because of the color, but because I knew that another worker would come later to paint and make the new boards indistinguishable from the old. These pieces of raw, freshly planed wood were an intolerable intrusion. As though one were trying to graft living cells onto dead, decayed flesh, or to fit a round white leg onto a flat, blackened mummy. I didn't want the destruction to be altered. But now I can't tell the new boards from the old. The evil has absorbed the new tissue and saturated it with its rotten essence.

The gravel crunches again under my feet as I pass over to

the wooded side, toward the entrance to the most mysterious part of the dwarfish building. But neither the gravel nor the bright Sunday afternoon can explain why the massive oven now seems so unprepossessing to me. With its doors thrown open, it looks like the jaws of a stocky fish, of a pudgy blind dragon with a shelf on wheels set before it so platters of food can be slipped into its deep gullet all the more quickly. But our dying took place far from this iron monster, and aside from the very few who carried stretchers here, no one ever had a chance to see it. Back in those days, Tolya and I would go only as far as the ground-level room underneath it. Yes, we felt a breath of the impending end from those powerful jaws, but more than anything that breath came from the clammy depths of our realization of utter captivity. When bodies finally appeared before the head of the metal whale, they were so dehydrated that they resembled driftwood twisted into bizarre shapes. By then they had fully merged with its terror, and if there was a deranged look in the wide-open eyes, it wasn't from the roiling harrows of this open trap. For such eyes had long since fixed on a limitless abyss and turned to glass.

But the visitors here are moved by the sight of this huge maw. They stand before a machine of destruction that requires no effort of the imagination. They can *see*; there is no need for them to visualize according to the guide's description. They can touch the iron, or try to move one of the double doors made of two heavy layers of metal. The guide warns: Be careful not to get yourselves dirty, the oven has been greased. And it does glisten from the lubrication, like a retired machine proud of its long years of faithful service and dressed for a special occasion. A wave of tourists almost sweeps me along with it, and I retreat to the background. I think of how the guide warned them not to get themselves dirty. The use of that word, however appropriate, makes me grow even more remote from the crowd that fills the room. Through a loudspeaker the guide's words pursue me, though he still stands beside the oven. He speaks calmly, however, without passion or desire to upset the crowd, and I find that his presentation is factual. Up there, in that huge cubical boiler suspended above the oven, water was heated for the showers that you can see through the window to your right. A group of young people presses around the window, while I remember the sensation of foam, yellow from the gritty soap, washing off our skin. Again I marvel at how oblivious I was to the way the water was heated, and at the fact that even that knowledge wouldn't have affected me. This insensitivity separates me from the crowd of Sunday sightseers. But it is also as if the dead, by their gift of a minute of hot water, had inducted me into their brotherhood, one holier than all the brotherhoods that religion has produced.

The voice from the loudspeaker explains that the long, bent instrument hanging from the wall was used by the stoker to even out the ashes as they settled, and that he used the rake to sweep them into a pile. The four large hooks that

jut from the beams behind the oven, the voice goes on, were
for secret hangings, while public hangings took place on a
gallows that we will see when we return to the camp's upper
level. So that's how they did it. I had always thought that
they hanged them from the showerheads. Probably someone
offhandedly said showerheads when Leif was examining a
group of young Poles, and that image stayed with me. Only
now do I realize how unlikely that was. Showerheads would
not have been solid enough for the job. But the practical
question of bent, black iron is insignificant beside the fear
driving a human being night and day. How André suffered,
until we were evacuated to Dachau, and even there the fear
occasionally overcame him, the fear that a proof of his ac-
tivities in the resistance would catch up with him. Every
time someone was led down the steps toward the ovens,
André would turn paler than usual, he would forget that he
was a good and self-sacrificing doctor, and stand helpless and
frail amid the chill that swept up from the lowest terrace.
As a doctor he had been present many times when the SS
brought groups of young men for examination. *Entlassung.*
Ready to be released. Let go. Sent off. That was the real
meaning of the term. Sent off, for good. A doctor had to
verify that the prisoners to be released were in good health.
The young men would look up with reluctant, vacant eyes
while an SS officer vented his fury at the one missing his
right leg from the knee down. "Aren't you healthy? Don't
you want to be released?" Leif nervously fiddled with his

stethoscope. The entire comedy of death would take turns in his examination chair, and he would be powerless to change anything. Powerless to resist the order to examine them. That was why he was a doctor, wasn't it? André didn't care for Leif, but he too was powerless. Only the fellows who had access to the file of convalescents in block 2 were ever able—and rarely at that—to save any of the marked men. And in doing so they risked everything, for if they were found out, they would be the ones next marched down the steps to the hooks. Franc, a tall and winning idealist from Ljubljana, always resourceful, restless, and full of irrepressible wit, managed to save some. When the SS man came with his list of "releases," the feverish process of rescue began. For one, sometimes as many as two, but not often, since that could raise suspicion. It was done by slipping a tag marked with the condemned man's number onto the big toe of one of the corpses that were always lying on the washroom floor, waiting to be carried to the oven. The rescued man received a new name and number, and it was imperative that he be out of the camp with some work detail as quickly as possible. Many of the work brigades marched off to death, it's true, but at least one person had escaped the hooks. When the SS returned for their people, Franc had to work hard to keep from shaking. When the man's number was called, he would say, "*Gestorben.*" And the SS man would ask, "*Wann?*" To hide his nervousness, Franc would then show him the list of the dead. "Here are all the dates," he would say, and not until the SS man left would he realize that his sweat-soaked shirt was clinging to him and that he was shivering.

André probably knew nothing of this horrible, marvelous risk-taking, because in such matters the fewer conspirators there are, the better. But even if he knew, it would have made no difference.

The people now crowding the area between the oven and the back wall with the hooks will never learn about Franc, the tall, nervous boy from Ljubljana, or André, the French doctor, and yet it is touching to see how they look around this factory of death in confusion. I step into the corridor that runs the length of the barracks, and stop in the next room, but again I am surrounded by crowds childishly straining their necks to see the ashes in the red earthen pots. Early on these were provided only for people of German extraction, but even for them this privilege was short-lived; before long their ashes were scattered in the same places as those of ordinary Europeans. As I look at the small, coarsely ground chunks of bone that fill the pots, and see that a little button lies among them, the tour guide tells us how many heads must be shaved to produce one kilogram of hair usable for weaving blankets. These facts have no bearing on my memories, and I move slowly through the crowd toward the exit. The guide's calm voice accompanies me, though he still stands by the oven. This, he says through the loudspeaker, is the room where executions took place. Notice how the floor is gently sloped to allow the victims' blood to run off. In September 1944, one hundred and eight members of the Alsatian resistance perished in this room. Yes, he's talking about the one ninety-year-old man and all those women. I shove my way to the door, annoyed by the crowd and his voice, but when I reach the the next room, there he is beside me again with his explanations. This, as you see, is the dissecting table. A professor from the University of Strasbourg performed his vivisections and bacteriological experiments here, and he made a point of visiting the camp to observe the state of the deportees who received varying doses of gas in the gas chamber, some taking more, others less time to die.

I am outside, and think that I would rather be standing in front of the oven than by that table with its yellowed tiles, where you can almost see the rubber gloves lying and the refined hands that will soon pull them on. The oven, for all its crudity, is cleaner. The stoker who works it may be an oaf, he may be ignorant, but he is not necessarily cruel. Mankind, given its inclination to murder, given our delight in the suffering and blood of others, requires quite a number of gravediggers. Gravedigging is a profession like any other. But that red-gloved hand engendered a criminal atmosphere here that even now hovers over the yellow-tiled table in the middle of the room. I circle the barracks alone, and this is as it should be; I don't need people now. But I pick up their muffled talk. A woman's voice asks, "*Qu'est ce que c'est ça?*"

A man answers, "*Le four.*" The woman says, "*Les pauvres.*" All around me figures rise on tiptoe to see the ashes and ground bones in their earthen pots, and I think that human conscience awakens at a hopelessly slow pace. He said, "The oven." She, "Poor devils." Laconic, pregnant with meaning, you might think, yet her remark strikes me as the sigh of a woman who has just seen a car run over a cat. I know, it's unfair; her question in front of the iron monster's gaping jaws may have simply been to relieve the awkwardness of the situation. And I should take into consideration the fact that evil has not become a part of her daily life as it has for me. She does not have my memories, which shift inside me like algae when stagnant water is stirred.

The shadows of the dead are far away. But maybe they approach when darkness covers the mountain and the terraces are buried under snow, for there are no tourists then. When the shadows come, they do as they used to; they lay the dying down on their snowy biers, then stand in formation, not waiting for a man in boots to count them. In total silence they assess and weigh the messages that drift toward them from the noisy world of the living.

The cellar beneath the oven, a warehouse equipped with a rudimentary black iron lift. This is the Natzweiler morgue. I see Tolya and myself as we bring in Ivo; I see the black poles and the thick gray canvas of the stretcher. We heaved Ivo up and set him on top of the heap. I thought of the long tongs that would clamp around his neck when the brute eventually pulled him off. Ivo lay amid jutting ribs, hollow pelvises, sharp cheekbones, and skulls like bowling balls. His was the only face shaven, because I had finagled a razor somehow, from somewhere, and painstakingly scraped clean the hollows of his cheeks, so that at least in this respect he would be following our customs. On top of all those bones in their jaundiced skin, his face seemed to come alive, and he called to me, not to leave him with all those strangers after we had spent so much time together, for he and I went back to the cement cell beneath Oberdank Square. He kept calling, even as Tolya and I carried the empty stretcher up the steps. In the middle of the coarse canvas was a brown stain, from heaven knows what corpse months before. I listened, and Ivo reproached me for deceiving him with reassurances that the disease wouldn't take him, for being inexhaustibly cheerful, the way I would sit on his bunk and chat, as though he were a convalescent who after a long illness needed only to rest. I followed Tolya, hefting up the stretcher poles, because I was shorter than he and didn't want them to hit the stone steps. But even if they had, Tolya wouldn't have cursed, because he knew I had just said farewell to a countryman, and for a young Russian a countryman is a sacred thing. I felt as though I had buried my own father. I felt the great fragility we feel when we look upon the cold body of the man who sired us. It was as though a mole had gnawed through the taproot that connected my existence here among these fatal terraces with those other terraces on a steep hillside facing the sea. To the last I had truly believed that Ivo would pull through. Believed and deeply wished, because his ironic smile and gentle nature had woven a bond between us. Leif, learning of my defeat, assured me in a fatherly way not typical of him that Ivo would have succumbed in normal life, too. Perhaps, and yet Leif Poulson, my boss, remained somewhat indifferent. He was always indifferent when he wasn't dealing with his fellow Norwegians. Had it been a different patient, perhaps Leif would have found some sulfa somewhere. Not at the final stage of the disease, of course, but early on, when Ivo first took sick. I'm well aware that the sulfamides the doctors received were used up within two days. But if Leif had wanted, he could have found some sulfa. I should have pleaded with him then, stepped forth on Ivo's behalf. But sulfa was the last thing on my mind at the time, and Leif wasn't even sure what was wrong with Ivo. When Leif finally mentioned nephritis, Ivo was going. Sulfa might not have made any difference. It might have been a tubercular infection. I was too insignificant a player in camp politics for Leif to discuss this with me.

And now Ivo refuses to appear. I can't recall his face. The warehouse and the tongs are here, but to Ivo and me they have no relevance. I am alone, standing in shadow, which is warm from the July sun now shining on the other side of the barracks, on its right flank. Not until I look around in confusion do I realize how many things now come between Ivo and me: my sandals and light summer trousers, the ball-point pen I use to jot down the name of a thing I want to remember, the Fiat 600 waiting for me at the exit—the car in which I've driven past the warehouse in Rojan where Ivo once sold coal. I would have to forsake all worldly goods and put on wooden clogs to become worthy of his company again. Then Ivo would no longer be invisible, and he wouldn't reproach me for returning to the coastline of Trieste. Maybe he would even stop insisting that I not take pleasure in the tanned skin of the bathers, or that I turn a deaf ear to the music of the water lapping beneath the cliffs of the shore at Barkovlje.

I ran into Tomaž one day while I was trying to find Leif to get help for Ivo.

That summer the weather was perfect, but its perfection wasn't made for us. Now and then as one went down the steps, the eyes would drift to the distant valley soaking the sun's rays. Warmth shimmered over the peaceful, captive world, and we observed it as if through the aqueous lens of an inverted telescope. We had a wonderful view, but experienced none of the pleasure of a person admiring a panorama. We had been planted on this height not to feel connected to human scenery but, rather, to be shown how totally cut off from it we were. Even so, a furtive glance at the summer valley was heartening, for at the bottom we could see the white, triangular gable of a low building. It was a summer house, or else a sanatorium from which, so we thought, the patients had long since been evacuated. It was the only man-made object in the landscape, an improbable prow of a white ship between the mountains, a symbol of departure and motion. Then suddenly one day on that distant prow a small flag appeared, a red cross on a white field. This meant not only that there were people there but that they had become afraid. Like a light that flickers through the dim consciousness of a sleeper who slowly wakes. They were afraid of the Allies approaching Belfort, afraid of the Allied planes. And deep inside us a germ of hope stirred, though most of us refused to admit it for fear of damaging it with our crippled, clumsy thoughts. For the terraces on our hillside were still the same vineyards of death, and the harvesting in them did not stop. Stretcher bearers continued to haul their produce down to the lowest terrace, and from there the smoke rose and spread above the tarred barracks roofs.

Yet summer was a merciful season. Outside the barracks that housed those unfit for work, bodies could sit on the few available benches, the wood of their bones resisting the wood of the seats. Others stretched out in the dirt, partly for lack of benches, but mostly from exhaustion. When you press your head, chest, stomach, and legs against the ground, you get the delirious sense that you can soften the planet's hard crust and draw some life force from it. But then, overcome, you feel your own strength, the pitiful remnant of it, seeping

into the earth instead. There are other moments, when the
stink of the smoke keeps watch over the stretched-out legs.
Then, despite its longing for quiet, your heart rebels. You
fight the smell of scorched tallow, closing your mouth and
expelling the stench through your nostrils, as though to outwit a cloud of poisonous gas. But you can twitch your head
away for only so long, and it's no use forcing death out of
your lungs if you have to inhale it again, however slowly and
haltingly. So it's best not to think and to let your lungs adapt
to the low wavelength of destruction, the departure into
night and fog emblemed by the two large, red capital letters
on the backs and trousers of the Norwegians, Dutch, and
Frenchmen: N. N. *Nacht und Nebel.*

The flag in the valley cut like a lightning bolt through
the night and fog. This is why I was so anxious to find Leif.
I knew there was nothing he could do for Ivo, who had
already started raving and confusing tattered images of Trieste
with this prison world. But the changes the flag promised
made his death seem so unfair. Perhaps in the agitation of
sudden hope I also thought that Leif might be inspired by
the good news and come up with just the thing that would
save Ivo, produce the medicine he'd kept hidden for precisely
such an occasion. Before, I had found Leif in Block 11 con-
veying the news of the flag in the valley to his Norwegians.
He did it with little excitement, but I could see the light
dancing in his eyes, and the circle around him was affected,
particularly a tall old salt straight out of some Scandinavian

novel. The man was missing the unruly shock of gray hair
—his head was shaven—and there was no pipe in his mouth,
but you could tell this fjordless sailor hadn't given up the
hope of boarding a ship again. Leif, too, despite his white
hair and the stethoscope glinting against his striped jacket,
looked more like a captain than a doctor. He was invulner-
able, proud, manly, and the sight of him was like getting an
injection of resistance. As, for instance, on that evening
when the body of a young man was brought into the infirmary
after roll call and placed on the narrow tin operating table.
A rigid, motionless body that not long ago, when there was
still snow on the terraces, would have been taken straight
to the warehouse beneath the oven. A corpse, I thought, as
Leif, quiet and erect, unbuttoned the dirty striped jacket,
sliced the shirt open across the chest, and placed the funnel
of his stethoscope in different places on the left side. There
was no sign of life, no sound in the nickel-plated tubes in
his ears. Then he said, as if to himself, *"Man soll versuchen."*
He stepped back with dignity, broke off the end of an ampule
of Coramine, held a hypodermic needle in his right hand
while with the index and middle fingers of his left he gauged
the distance between the ribs, then inserted the needle
straight into the heart. For a physician in a hospital this was
not so unusual, but when a body thought to be dead starts
to wave its arms, catch its breath, and writhe, the layman
feels as if he were witnessing the resurrection of Lazarus. The
boy was alive. Later he would smile whenever Leif stopped

by his bunk, but smile vacantly, as though unsure why the doctor had summoned him back into the light.

No, Ivo couldn't be helped, he was beyond help. And I couldn't find Leif anyway. That's when a Norwegian medic told me about Tomaž. *"Kamerad Jugoslav,"* he said, which as often as not meant that the man was a Slovene from the littoral, because in a realm where everything is simple in the extreme, long explanations are a burden. Tomaž had a big capital I in the middle of his red triangle—he was captured as an Italian citizen—but insisted, as any Slovene would, that he was a Yugoslav. No Slovene wanted to be exterminated in this place as an Italian, for since the end of the First World War the Italian government had been trying to eradicate him on his native soil. And Istrian Croats too, like the Slovenes, resisted sharing the fate of a people whose country they had been annexed to against their will. The proximity to death removed all masks, and thus the Norwegian medic called Tomaž a Yugoslav, though it wouldn't matter when we went down to the terrace with the oven.

Tomaž was unlike anyone I had ever met. Unlike because of the excitement in his eyes, his unbridled talkativeness, his incredible, childlike faith. He was an abundance that refused to limit itself. A disposition that could never be sober yet that steadfastly remained as discerning as on the first day I met him. He couldn't have been much shy of fifty, yet he would smirk and stretch his arms along his body like a boy who has just been told that he can get up in a little while if he behaves.

Day after day he lies there beside the window, bits of straw slipping between the planks of the upper bunk and landing on his bedcover. Day after day he lies on his back, brushing the straw away with his fingers, looking as if, with the planks over his head, over his swollen body, he had been delivered in a crate. There is so much contagion beneath the cover that the very air seems contaminated, the forest and the whole mountain seized by rot. And yet his eyes look like two crystalline pools back home, and when he talks about the Canale in Trieste, or Stockmarket Square, or the square by Rusi Bridge, he squints like a fisherman gazing up at clouds backlit by the sun. He's glad that I've let myself be caught up in his game, and delighted by the unexpected visit, as I try to gauge if he has any idea how enormously good-natured he is in this place of boundless poison. It's just like him to pull off the cover, pat his bloated stomach, and compare himself to a pregnant woman, assuring me that the swelling will subside, then to cover himself again, the white flag in the valley fluttering in his eyes all the while.

To be sure, others felt a new spark of life since the planes began flying overhead. The whips kept falling on their shoulders and on their bony arms raised to protect their bare skulls, but when the shouts stopped and the zebra-striped rags had filled the barracks at dusk, all eyes turned to the sky. The bodies, bent or crouching, craned their emaciated necks. Packed tight, they followed the course of the huge silverfish caught in the white net of the clouds. The drone in the sky caused a mysterious shiver in the rib cage; this inner echo was especially strong at night, as the body lay stretched out. It grew to a rumble. "It's started," someone said half in sleep. "This'll get them out of bed in Munich!" another voice said in a jeering murmur. Starving limbs rolled over and pulled the covers up tight, throats swallowed with pleasure the little saliva that was left, and ears no longer heard the howling of the dogs on the black mountainside. A flickering hope, a ray of sun, but it soon died under a thick layer of ash.

Not so with Tomaž. His playfulness never left him. He guarded it, tended it, surrounded me with it. He told me about the bridge he and his son blew up to stop an advancing German column, and his bright eyes held me captive, the eyes of a visionary who wanted me to be invincible too, so I could receive from him the Istrian red wine he planned to bring to my house in Trieste. A barrel. No, two barrels. Oh, if only he could sip some of that red wine now, he would recover fast. He'll bring the barrels right to my doorstep, he says as he casts a vague look at the rows of bunks. Beside him someone moans under a blanket, someone else gurgles, and a pair of eyes above a checkered sheet cast a half-imploring, half-defiant look at him, two unmoving, glassy spheres in a body being carried out on a stretcher. "They're always carrying them out," Tomaž says, but in the same breath adds that he could get better if only he had some wine. He'll bring me two barrels, that's what he'll do. He's glad his son escaped into the mountains, and it's clear now that his mischievousness is for me, and for his son whom he will make invincible too with the light of his eyes. I didn't understand him then, and I still don't. It's too easy to say that Tomaž was trying to cheat death with his high spirits and tricks. Transporting himself to his Istria, where he drew healing nourishment from the ground. It's too easy to say that he used his loquaciousness to cover the doubts that beset him inside like gargoyles. How was it, then, that his tongue never hesitated, that he never flagged, that he always kept his balance, always managed to stay above water? Perhaps he was a phenomenal actor, an actor who never once stumbled in his race with death, and never once removed his mask. Not even at night. Had I visited him at night (I don't believe I did), I'm sure that then, too, I would have found the same smile waiting for me.

As we started preparing for evacuation, I worried about how we would load all the Tomažes onto trucks and cattle cars, leaving the terraces now free of barking dogs and smoke. I worried about how we would then unload all the Tomažes before the minarets of the new faith. I worried about Tomaž, that his heavy body would prevent him from running toward freedom. So I kept quiet while he talked, talked more than usual. He said that in Dachau we would at least be closer to home. This angered me, as had all the rumors earlier that

Vosges resistance fighters would liberate us, or the prediction that paratroopers would rescue us. But I kept my anger to myself, and Tomaž sat securely amid his Istrian vineyards, far away from us. But that's not right, I thought. You can't be here *and* there in the world of the living, Tomaž, death doesn't allow it. You can't be in the salt marshes around Sečovlje, or opening the drawers of the massive chest in your ancient farmhouse and enjoying the crisp smell of coarse linen. You can't. I glanced around to make sure I wasn't following him, to make sure I didn't hear the goat braying out back or see the heifer rubbing its neck against a hayrack. The red wine kept flowing freely in his cellar, kegs of it, barrels, a flood of red wine we would both be bathing in, swimming in before long. But you shouldn't, Tomaž. Look, there goes a stretcher right past your bunk. Death is jealous, Tomaž. At my silence he grew serious for a moment, perhaps afraid that he had offended me. When I explained that I had been thinking that we needed to do all we could to stay clear of the crematorium, he brightened up again. He rubbed his hands like a good-hearted landowner who despite a serious illness has just concluded an important deal with his neighbor. "At least in Dachau we'll be closer to home!" he repeated. He wanted my address, but shook his head when I tore a sheet of paper from my notepad. No, he wanted me to write it on one of the planks above his head so he could have it before his eyes at all times. And as I drew the long, spindly letters, like sketching the pier of San Carlo and both belltowers of the Greek Orthodox church, he whispered in my ear that he would bring the wine. I could hear the sound of the wagon rolling down my quiet street, and the jangling carts of the two milkmaids from Smarje and Koštabone, both just off the steamship from Koper. And yet I was sitting on the wooden frame of his bunk and touching his shoulder. Perhaps he thought it was his son touching him, because it was as if I were touching a father I would never forget. His eyes sparkled with satisfaction, and he winked and raised his head to the plank above him. "I'll learn it by heart," he said, meaning the address.

On a later morning the Dachau parade grounds are an enormous garbage dump, with countless shovels heaving paper, wet rags, broken clogs, and filthy striped bundles onto it out of washroom windows. Among the mattresses that cover the large field are unwrapped paper bandages, worn wooden spoons, and a knife fashioned in prehistoric times. Mattresses with wet stains, empty, lacking the forms that made the indentations in them. Mattresses with naked bodies. Bodies with wounds. Female genitalia with hard, swollen labia. Decomposing labia eight inches wide. More rubbish. More clogs. More heaps of wet, filthy zebra skins laid low by typhus. Next to them, bodies still functioning, undressing on the mattresses. A bandage unraveling like the thread of the insatiable Fates. A bony hand refusing to let go of its wooden spoon. Ribs protruding under scaly skin. These bodies were not sent to the right, they were the ones that made it to the barracks. Along the edge is a long row of empty pallets from which the dead are being removed before they start rotting beneath the burning sky, which gives no sign of falling. In a narrow gorge between two barracks everything is peaceful and orderly. Inside, a doctor wearing glasses and rubber gloves is slicing open a body. Water runs onto the table, rinsing it almost inaudibly. He is in a white smock, speaks Czech, and for each corpse has to find the cause of death. He works skillfully, fast, as if he doesn't need to rummage through the entrails, as if he knows in advance. He works fast because there is no end to the bodies. He has been working since early morning. Now he sews, shoving in the thick needle and weaving a braid from crotch to chin. Gaping jaws, yellow teeth, boardlike abdomens. Only one is white and swollen. *"Dein Kamerad Jugoslav,"* the Norwegian medic says. I have been looking at the boards that make up the barracks wall behind his head. They are like the planks above Tomaž, only wider, and in place of the stretcher moving past the bunks there is a wheelbarrow with a long tin trough. Beside it, a tin cover. I look at Tomaž's eyes at the end of the braid that goes up his midsection. The eyes, open to the empty sky, seem on the verge of smiling. See what a braid they've woven me, he is trying to say. I remember how his eyes resisted the dark in the cattle car. As in the other closed cars, there was a swarm of bodies less feeble and less wasted than his shifting day and night, especially night. They stepped over his body, on his neck and stomach, but his eyes continued to pierce the darkness, as if to invalidate it.

The morning sun shines on the traveling sealed crates. A ray of light hits the ceiling of the car, illuminating the boards over his head as the wheels count the joints: closer to home, closer to home, closer to home. His eyes stare so intently that they don't notice the planks being removed and replaced with the vault of senseless blue that arches over his wise and fatherly head.

I don't remember whether I thought of him the morning we were getting ready to leave, or as I paused at the top of the steps to look at the terraces stretching down the hill. They were deserted. The barracks still stood in pairs on either side of each terrace. But the silence was new. It basked in the gold of the September sun, and urged the mountains around to regain their old shapes. The pine forest, that dark-green shield that concealed the bunker and barracks and oven, was stirring. And the heart stirred, awakening after an eternity of hiding from destruction, to peer out like the snout of a lizard from a rock crevice. What will become of the terraces when the last truck leaves? Will the forest rustle and rain pour in springtime, and will snow bury these steps cut into the hillside in winter? Will the sun rise in summer again in the mountains? And in fall, as now? What of the thousands of clogs that have stood in the snow during interminable roll calls? And the mailman from Padrice who had to be carried to roll call, his striped trousers slipping down to his ankles as he was laid out on the snow while the SS man did his count. Who was then picked up after roll was over and carried down here, where tourists are milling now. What will become of him? Or of the shaven heads pelted by the rain, and the eyes that are still glassy—hunger hasn't sucked them dry yet, because thick bone protects them from the drought that will drain all other parts of the body first. What will become of the eyes, that with their freshness most defy this continent of skeletons? They turn into two turbid pools just before the end. Will there be a trace of any of this once these steps are deserted? With such questions did I attempt to leap into the future.

The steps gripped me like a vision of a doomed Mexican ruin, but work demanded that I go to the barracks, so I started down the stairs again. Then I saw the men who had given up waiting for help and had risen from their mattresses on their own. Or maybe it was the unusual silence that got them out into the sun—frail phantoms whose bare feet made no sound. Naked, their shirts barely reaching their hollow crotches, they groped their way over the narrow terrace. Flapping their arms to keep their balance, like blinded birds whose feathers had been singed off. They went to the steps and began straining uphill, as if to escape the fire that would have ravaged the last cells of their bodies. They hung onto the steps and crawled up on all fours, spindly water striders, scorched, knock-kneed spiders, as if each excruciating move was the last. Then followed a long pause in the sun and silence. But perhaps the thin creatures feared that the sun too was an enemy, wanting to suck the last drop from them, because the stiff limbs suddenly reached for the next step and seized it, then rested again, and above one was another crawling toward the upper terrace, and above him yet another, a whole row of crawlers raising their bare turtlelike heads in their effort to leave the place of evil.

Tolya ran past me, carrying a stretcher over one shoulder. "*Davay!* Come on!" he called out, in irritation because I rested while he was working just as hard as he once did at the threshing machine of his kolkhoz. "I'm coming," I said, thinking I should take the steps on the right-hand side, so as not to get in the way of the crawlers. But then a squealing came from the path that ran along the far side of the barracks, a rhythmic noise in the silence, threatening because that was a path never used. The barbed wire ran beside it, and normally no one went near the wire. The squealing ascended slowly and with difficulty up the hill. Then a wheelbarrow emerged from behind the barracks, and another. Who thought of using wheelbarrows instead of stretchers, which were always in short supply? Now they were moving past, part of a column of exhausted workers returning from the earth's depths, a procession of miners who had laid their picks and shovels in the barrows, except that instead of mining tools the limbs of excavated storks were jutting out of the triangular crates. One of the skeletons still wore a shirt, its ride in the wheelbarrow all the more grotesque for that. The shaven bird-heads bob up and down, their mouths open, as though trying to snap up flies, but they can't because they're jostled by the ride. I don't remember exactly what I was thinking then. Probably that we wouldn't have to carry them now that someone had thought of using wheelbarrows instead. And that a treacherous silence would descend on the mountain one hour from now, when we had gone. No photograph would be hanging in the air. The silence would cover everything, horde everything for itself, including this procession, the squealing, the ever more distant sound of a rusty spit.

This evacuation would turn out to be the mildest I would witness. We even had musical accompaniment. The doors on both sides of our car had been left open, allowing a steady succession of the autumn countryside's forgotten images to float past in their frame. The wheels clanked against the rail joints; and speed was an incomprehensible novelty. I sat in a corner with Albert. We could barely carry on a conversation for the music's volume. Paul playing trumpet, Pierre the violin, someone else the accordion. You would have thought the war was over and we were being carried home. Closer to home, and this was the beginning of the end, Albert maintained, though I tried to refute him. "You know where they're taking us, don't you?" I said. He wasn't in the least perturbed; if the Allies were already in Belfort, that meant they had to move us somewhere else. "Fine," I said. "But these wheels rumbling underneath us are taking us *away* from the Allies. Besides, in Dachau there are far more powerful jaws for wagons of bones like ours." "What?" he asked, because Paul had just reached a frenzied high note on his trumpet. "They have huge ovens there," I said. But he shrugged, as if to say we'd have burned on our mountain, too, if we had stayed. Albert had a broad face, the kind that exudes trust, but in our world this quality of his had worn thin over time. I reminded him, somewhat maliciously, that he'd been an optimist in summer, too, and that by July we'd had it with his predictions. But his face, a full moon unaware of its benign smile, didn't relent. "They are in Belfort now, my friend," he said impishly, and I was relieved when Daniel called him over.

Paul, too, had faith. He was puckering into the trumpet's mouthpiece like an outlandish angel with short-cropped blond hair. His brother Pierre believed, and so did the accordion player. They played on, refusing to tire as they stood by the door, the notes pouring out of the racing railroad car and onto the September fields like defiant golden seed. They played without a break, Pierre with them on his violin, though it was such a delicate instrument, easily muffled by the trumpet and accordion. Of the three men he was the most gentle. And they were not the only musicians. A regular chamber orchestra assembled officially each evening before the barking of German shepherds pierced the mountain night. But Paul also played for himself, while our bodies stretched out in the barracks quickly in order to stop the desperate pleas of our starving tissues with fitful sleep. If a stretcher went down the steps just then, the spindly corpse received a few bars of Mozart as its last rites.

Paul sat in the open doorway, his legs dangling out, and he swayed with his trumpet right and left, and raised it to the sky. The train's speed teased and excited us, without promising anything. But a dim future was more encouraging than the captive certainty of the realm of nothingness. Perhaps that was why Paul was blasting away. I don't know. I was no less skeptical now than I had been when everyone talked about the resistance. Some shadow of evil must have fallen on me in childhood to rule out even a weak glimmer of hope. I could only think of how much more difficult it was going to be to unload the cars, because neither the wheelbarrow passengers nor the lone crawlers could move now on their own. I looked at André standing in the corner opposite with Dr. Senet and other doctors and medics, and imagined how many hours he had endured watching the SS march men to the hooks beside the oven. Seeing himself in every group led there. He was listening to Senet now, but it was clear that his mind was elsewhere, perhaps wondering whether or not he should hope that the files get hopelessly mixed up during the move. Paul kept playing as the fields undulated past him, the colors splashing his feet. The sun's rays were caught by the strings of Pierre's violin. They must know where we're going, I told myself. That's why Paul is blowing so hard. As if in answer to this thought, Paul puffed his cheeks more, played his fingers over the valves, and pointed the horn at the sun. The SS men by the door gripped their rifles tighter, and Dr. Senet interrupted what he was saying to turn his distinguished white-haired but shaven head toward the door.

Our evacuation from Harzungen was abrupt, but in a different way. We found ourselves amid empty barracks and a silence gripping the cobblestone paths that ran between them. It was as if we were in a remote village that everyone had fled before the lava poured in. The April sun glinted pink in the square panes atop the wooden tower that held a guard and machine gun, while tongues of flame rose against the sky over Nordhausen, surrounding us with the feeling of apocalypse. We were with six hundred patients in the two barracks of the infirmary. Everyone who could walk had long since left, God knows where. We were the last, as always, and we stopped carrying the corpses to the bin behind the barracks because there was no one to transport them to Dora. We had to bury them. Vaska and a helper were digging a pit between the barracks. In the tower above them the guard joked. He had lowered the window in front of his machine gun and was explaining something. He looked like a man unaccustomed to human speech after a long isolation. Vaska ignored him. He had dug deep into the pit now and was sweating, and he tossed a Russian curse at the guard's mother. The guard lowered the window some more, pleased that the ditchdigger seemed to enjoy his wit. Maybe the deserted camp and the approaching end of the Reich had awakened a spark of humor in him as he sat in his glass house.

Where were we to start, the ten of us, with all these invalids, half of whom couldn't get out of bed? On their mattresses we moved them into the hallway so they could be loaded on the truck that would stop at the barracks entrance. They lay side by side and head to foot against corridor walls, allowing a narrow path down the middle. First in line were the ones with gas gangrene. They waited patiently, following us with their eyes as we carried past the blue-and-white checkered bags stuffed with paper bandages. Then we brought out those who had lost all curiosity and were simply a pair of cheekbones jutting out of a ragged heap on the floor. Some moaned in an attempt to get attention. But no one had time for them. And it was coming down to the pinch. So many mattresses still filled the corridor, and we were told that the truck and trailer would take only two more loads. It's best not to think about it, you tell yourself. Just then one died, and the doctor told me to call Vaska and make sure the corpse was buried. "All right," I said, "but the Czech kid in my room is on the edge." I went to find Vaska, and the two of us carried the body out into the yard. Vaska shoveled dirt onto him, while behind his glass panes the guard in the tower shone red from the fire in the sky over Nordhausen, and I thought about the doctor going into my room, towel in hand. Then Vaska said, "If you want me to keep digging, bring me some bread." And it seemed right for me to go fetch bread that corpses had left behind. "I'll be back in a minute," I said and ran into the barracks. I hesitated at the door, afraid that what I might find would be too awful, but also half hoping that my delay would give them time to get it over with. I told myself that surely the doctor would know what his professional ethics dictated. Maybe it's best to ease the body's departure, especially since all the young Czech could do was open his mouth from time to time and pucker his lips like a beached fish unsure whether the sea existed anymore. As I pushed on the handle, the door opened only a crack before someone kicked it shut again from inside. That was the medic, who then called out for me to wait. I wanted to push open the door, but hesitated. Wouldn't it be better for the boy to rest under a layer of soft earth that Vaska had dug, than to die on a truck under a pile of mattresses and bodies? I moved away. The patients lying on their rotting beds on the floor mumbled something I couldn't understand. The doctor came out of the room and said the boy had died and I should get Vaska. Instead, I ran to the boy's bunk to see if there was anything I could do. His rib cage was still rising and falling; he was still gasping through swollen lips. At first I felt enormous relief, but broke out in a sweat when I touched his cheek and saw a red bruise around his neck that hadn't been there before. The Czech's young body had been failing all through the spring, and its long stubbornness had been an unexpected consolation for me, a kind of deliverance from my agonized doubts about helping a person die. But now, as I watched the mouth open for air at greater and greater intervals, I decided that the one who helped these tortured bodies reach the end was doing good. Though I was not sure about the doctor's motive. Perhaps he did it not out of any compassion for his fellow man but to reduce the number of bodies that would have to be loaded onto the truck. In the hallway I said to him, to take revenge, "The boy's still breathing." Except I said this in a low voice, as we were walking between the rows of mattresses, so it's possible he didn't hear me. I don't know.

The truck was backing up to the entrance. Knobby elbows were lifting themselves up from the floor. Bodies somehow found the strength to stagger on their stick legs alongside Vaska, Pierre, and me as we led them out. The air was saturated with the stench of dysentery and the pus that had discolored their paper bandages. This was nothing new. What was unusual was the noise we medics made. We were encouraging each other, because we were so few. One grabbed a mattress across the middle and lifted it along with the bones on it. Another dragged a mattress behind him. And those who were arranging the bodies up in the truck set the first of them on the floor beside each other. On this layer they quickly put a second. There was no time to lose. No time to pay attention to the feeble movements of those layers. Only one died as we loaded, and Vaska had to carry him behind the barracks. The young Czech, still alive, is at the bottom of a mountain of bodies, I thought, and felt less angry with the doctor. We put the bandages in their slip covers on top of everything, and the guards surrounded the two trucks and started shouting. The driver honked the horn in exasperation, because now we were missing only Vaska and the man who had gone with him around the barracks. We climbed up and sat on the edge where there was still some room, while Vaska and his helper came back and tied the two stretchers made of unfinished wood and wire mesh to the sides, so that the truck looked like a fire engine with ladders. Finally we were on our way.

The truck bounded down the road and through the forest in the direction of the huge fires that Allied airplanes had lit. Nordhausen. That was where Mladen got sick, I thought, trying to block out the wailing inside the truck. Night had fallen, and I couldn't see anything. The truck shook like a wooden bowl. I tried to focus on what the medics were saying to each other, to shut out the chorus of moans. In my imagination I could see the bodies in a monstrous threshing machine—knees jammed into mouths, the bony fin of a rear end under another's chin, a side wedged into a crotch, and stick legs in a tangled mass while the truck shudders from the cold like some living creature. Again I tried to collect my thoughts, and as the forest darkly followed the road, I pondered the mystery of this German land. Then a jolt, and all arms and legs joined to make a single body with a multitude of white, shining eyes and one mouth that groaned as a spring complains before it merges again with the hum of the engine. I thought about the chain around my neck, the owner of that chain, Mladen. But my thoughts of him were really no different from the picture in the dark before me. In Dachau Mladen avoided watching during autopsies, but later in Dora we watched as the knife disassembled his heart. No, it's no good thinking about Mladen, I told myself, or the fact that I have his chain. He was carted away and thrown onto a smoldering heap on the hilltop in Dora. And the young Czech, there must have been thirty bodies pressing down on him. He couldn't possibly be still breathing. Yes, it would have been better for him to be at rest in the earth. The doctor had acted realistically, wisely, and I had been too emotional. The medics behind me were discussing how we would all have to stick together at the station in order to set up an emergency room in one of the cattle cars, in order to survive and help others do the same. But then, at the station, where there were other trucks and the train was already waiting for us, it wasn't easy to stay together. We were assaulted by shouts from all sides. The beams of flashlights darted this way and that as we pulled bundles and bodies off the truck in the dark. Some of the bodies slid off our wire stretchers onto the ground.

We worked feverishly through the night, a blood-red sky over us, and when light finally streaked across the horizon again, we could see bodies still being pulled from the trucks by the head. As one bearer bent over to drag a body to the train, a mattress fell off the truck and flattened him. The guards kept wielding their bludgeons and kicking as they ran from the trucks to the train and back again. We had to remain calm as they cursed and shoved us into different cars. When they moved on, we got back out and climbed into a car where the other medics had already gathered. Finally we managed to carry all our bundles of bandages into that car. As always in life, you had to know what you wanted, you had to have a plan and be able to follow it despite panic and insanity. It isn't easy to act in a muddled crowd, struck one instant by a beam of light and the next by a bullwhip. But the most terrible thing was the bodies being dragged across the platform. It's lucky they were unconscious. Some stiff as boards, some that flopped and buckled as they were pulled through the chaos of running shadows.

How many days did that journey last? Six? Seven? Time had long since lost the meaning that the rotation and convergence of heavenly bodies give it. The end of night meant only that we would see each other again. The morning sun shone on nothing but a long line of moving or standing train cars. An unsurveyable chain of open crates of two-legged cargo, with only the German sky for a roof. We traveled for half a day, then stopped for an age, then set off in the opposite direction, then stopped and waited. The train halted once in a meadow, where we took an afternoon, evening, and night to bury one hundred sixty bodies, with Janoš directing the work. It was the first time in many months, not counting the few days before our departure from Harzungen, that our skeletons weren't sent to the ovens. The first two cars—the two behind the engine—were designated as the morgue. Unpleasant work, and yet these burials were a kind of pledge that the remote world of the living was approaching. There were no barracks and no barbed wire, only a meadow that the April sun flooded with a light that bore no resemblance to the cold lamps over autopsy tables. Even though our twenty-five or thirty cattle cars had been a week without food, and the two cars nearest the engine were filling up rapidly, there was consolation in the fact that sun, sky, and nature were free again and boundless.

Janoš, too, must have sensed this. Though he had worked all night, he hopped out of the car robust and limber, as though new life had entered him. The early-morning light and Janoš's example made me get up also, though I would have liked to stay under my blanket in the corner of the car. "Help me," he said. A young Pole was standing outside the door nursing his gray right arm with his left hand while Janoš examined it. The Pole was thin, about fifteen years old, head shaven, with a greenish pallor from not having eaten for five days and six nights. The SS had been shooting earlier, because some of the people from our car had made a dash for a car full of potatoes on the adjoining track. The boy had been among them and taken a bullet through the forearm. "Look how dirty you are," Janoš said testily, as if the whole world would be set right if the wounded arm were clean. He poured some disinfectant into a dish and gave it to me to hold. "What a ragamuffin you are," he grumbled, while the boy, all gray and green, shook slightly, his sparse beard jutting out. God knows if he still has a mother, I thought, and if he does, it's just as well that she can't see him now. I was pleased that we'd had the presence of mind to take along the bottles, dishes, and necessary equipment. I liked Janoš. He was not the person I'd known in camp—not arrogant anymore—and those boots of his, the ones that had compounded the bad impression he made, military boots that no one else had, now made him seem healthy and vigorous. Who knows how he came by that footwear. No doubt his camp history was colorful, but that lost all meaning now, as he grumbled at the boy in such a fatherly way. When a bony-faced and grim Unterscharführer walked past, Janoš changed instantly. He turned and asked the German to come and look at the arm. "So early at work?" the bony face said, grinning. "What nonsense is this?" Janoš exploded. "And for two potatoes, when they haven't eaten in five days." The Unterscharführer told him to watch himself, but he was also confused, partly because he hadn't expected such an attack, and partly because the SS always had a certain degree of respect for the medics, amazed that we should bother with the invalids created by the world of the crematoria. "Why let them out of the cars if they're just going to be shot at?" Janoš called after the SS man, who walked away smirking. The end was in the air, and maybe the man felt instinctive satisfaction that among these bodies silently indicting his nation with their dying, one delivered the indictment out loud. Perhaps it was even the smirk of a man who could already hear the rifle shots as he stood against a wall. "If it doesn't hurt, he's finished," Janoš said while he disinfected the arm as if it belonged to his little brother. The boy didn't flinch. He had lost all sensation and all thought. If they had given him a raw potato to chew on, I thought, he might have noticed his wound. The forearm was in two pieces, like a flail in a leather joint that lets it bend in any direction. Janoš bandaged it with a strip of white paper, with surprising tenderness, and as we lifted the boy into the car, he let loose at the poor wretches lying on the floor and saying they didn't want the boy there because he had dysentery. "I'll give you dysentery!" he shouted. It's true, I had known only one half of the man and had judged him by that half, I thought as I lay back down, wrapping myself in my blanket, because I was cold and my legs were weak. Then Janoš did something incredible: he produced paper and black polish and began to shine his boots. One must be strong and clever to be able to mock destruction, to slap death in the face, to vault like that out of its all-powerful kingdom. A kind of courage we'd long since abandoned. "What's the occasion?" one of the medics called out to him. "Got an inspection?" But Janoš just mumbled and smiled, tucking his striped jacket in at the waist.

I pulled the cover to my head for warmth, and soon I wasn no longer thinking about Janoš. I could hear the young Pole shivering under his short blanket in the opposite corner, and muffled groans near the open door. Two SS men were standing there, chewing on rubbery sausages. Slowly, deliberately they cut them into small pieces as pairs of eyes stared from under blankets. One of the Germans was a recruit in a baggy uniform, and the other wore glasses and might have been a postman in civilian life. There was no doubt that they felt uncomfortable around us, that they were new at this business. The car reeked of diarrhea, and here and there one could hear a loud rattling in chests. Some spat, some relieved themselves on a tarpaulin. Later, when one was wrapped up in the tarpaulin and carried to the cars behind the engine, his balled fist still clutched the edge of the canvas. Absently, machinelike, the two SS men raised bread and the pieces of sausage to their mouths. Sorry witnesses, I thought, and listened to the noise beneath the car. It was the scraping of an emaciated body leaning against a wheel. Most couldn't squat anymore and had to stand with head bowed by the railway cars. I could hear the arms gripping the metal wheel, the shaven head bumping against the floor of the car. Someone standing outside the door spoke to one of the SS men. *"Wer?"* the recruit asked, while the postman said that it couldn't be. *"Das geht nicht. Das geht nicht."* I looked out from under my blanket and saw the dismay on the postman's face, the sausage dangling pink in his hand. The prisoner at the door described how Janoš had shouted that there would be no shooting over potatoes, and how he kept shouting even after he had been hit and was lying on the ground. Yes, in the camp we had misjudged him. A person brimming with life feels the barbed wire around him differently. We had reproached him for occasionally sunbathing behind the barracks in summer, as though he was mocking the bodies withering around him. No, I told myself, this couldn't be, Janoš would be coming back any minute to ask how the boy was. "Are you sure it was Janoš?" the postman said when the prisoner at the door told him about the bullet in the head. I looked at Janoš's blanket next to mine. Who knows why he liked me. Maybe because we were the only two Slav medics. When at a stop we had hauled an old iron stove from a bombed-out train into our car, and he boiled a few bread crumbs and some grass in a banged-up tin can, he shared this soup with me. Then somebody said that he was being carried past, and even the SS men watched respectfully as two men in zebra stripes were indeed carrying something wrapped in a gray blanket, with no head or boots showing. A short body, so it must have been Janoš. Then I saw a man with a machine gun walking behind the modest procession, and I lay back again and pulled the blanket over my eyes. The April air was sharp, and I could feel the cold creeping into me. The two cars behind the engine were empty now that Janoš had spent the night directing the burial of all the corpses. He would be lying there alone.

Time moved slowly, and it was an eternity before we reached our destination, which was Celle. When we stopped alongside the higher platform that most stations have for freight trains, my thoughts wandered back to the tracks that run out of the free port of Trieste, where ages ago cattle cars just like these would set out before daybreak to a din that echoed off the warehouses. But here was total silence. It was noon, and the stillness hung over the countryside like poison gas. The guards, like machines, didn't shout, they simply watched the bodies crawl out of cars, or listened to occasional cries from those unable to move from their dim corners because they were too weak. I would have had to carry them —it wasn't enough for them to lean on me. But I didn't have the strength. I tried to shut my ears to their pleas, but my conscience wouldn't let me. I went back to encourage a man who had crawled out of the car on all fours and was sitting by the door, the awful stillness of the day condensing in his wide-open eyes. And I hesitated, perhaps in the fear that his exhaustion would delay me and we would be doomed together. Who can tell whether a person is selfish by nature or he is selfish as the result of his organism's weakness. Meanwhile the guards assured us that trucks would pick up everyone left lying in the long string of railroad cars—but how were we to believe them?

Our hobbling herd moved forward slowly, dissolving,

dropping its dehydrated, useless substance into the ditch beside the road. But no one finished off the fallen. The guards shrugged, as if they had received a mysterious revelation that no pistol or rifle shot would have meaning beneath this pale, condemned April sun. Because now death resided not just in the two cars nearest the engine, not just in birdlike ankles that had lost their wooden clogs along the way; it was present also in the single soldiers crossing the low hills and lazily, almost dreamily pursuing abandoned horses from a distance. All the steel and tank divisions notwithstanding, this lunatic vagabond cavalry fit the speechless scene of disintegration. We prisoners, who until now had been accustomed to seeing the image of negation in ourselves, in the features of walking skeletons, were now part of the broader panorama of a country coming apart. And this brought new energy into our stumbling legs. A group of Belgians who had been concealing a public prosecutor from Antwerp now hoisted him up on their shoulders and carried him around like a starved Gandhi on a wooden litter. Dust billowed up from beneath the soles of this procession, as a formation of Allied planes flew low over the hills and stray horses. The unexpected thunder was first a jolt, an echo of the inevitable end, then a convulsion of the earth as it was churned up by the falling scepter of an enraged god. We hardly noticed that we were entering a courtyard. The guards screamed at us, and we had to squat or lie down on the rough ground. To the left there was a gasoline pump, and beside it a pile of metal drums. This meant that we weren't at the entrance to yet another way-station with an oven but in front of an abandoned garrison for motorized units. I lay in the dust and imagined a bomb peeling away from a metal hull and releasing proud flames from the drums of gasoline. But the fliers of course could see the orphaned striped dots that covered the ground like the zebra carrion. When the rumbling stopped, we rose again, and our faces were no longer vacant, but the faces of Gypsies who even without wagons or fire could sense, doglike, the nearness of human habitation, which was two-storied military buildings that stretched at large, regular intervals across a rut-filled field. We hurried to occupy them, since a stone building promised undreamed-of safety to us who had lived so long in wooden barracks and cattle cars. All able bodies began to take the empty rooms by storm. Hands clutched at doorframes feverishly, as of wrecked sailors who finally touch dry land. There was much running up and down of stairs, jostling, the greedy staking out of abandoned bunks, rummaging through empty drawers, and the overturning of empty trunks. We were creatures who had forgotten what private property was, and in our frenzy of possession even our hunger diminished in importance.

Once again the medics were the only ones with a plan amid the confusion: we determined that one building should be the hospital, or rather a haven for the emaciated and dying. It is possible that this decision was dictated by our own instinct for self-preservation, but if so, it had nothing to do with any law of the survival of the fittest. Concern for one's fellow man needn't derive from selfish calculation—or from altruism, for that matter. It may be an organic need, like breathing or the exercise of thought. It may have to do with self-preservation only in the sense that work is above all a way for man to escape himself. Despite all the deaths there was still quite a crowd, and we had responsibilities, tasks: the relocation of bunk beds from room to room, the search for mattresses, the division of rooms into wards for edema, for gangrene, for dysentery, and of course for the sticklike mummies standing motionless in the corridors, oblivious to all around them. And then the disposition of the bodies and their proper burial. Lying still was the best medicine, in lieu of all the medicine we didn't have, the best even when the body was beyond hope, for it was the most appropriate position for that gentle slide into emptiness, when veins and muscles had dried into thongs of barely clinging vine that no longer transmitted pain. Worse even than the lack of food—some of our patients turning their eyes toward me as hatchlings turn their beaks, especially the ones with edema, who indeed resembled hatchlings with their swollen, sausagelike eyelids—was the complete absence of all the ritual appurtenances of the medical art. All we had were paper bandages, alcohol, and big ampules of glucose. No one knew why there had been so much of the sugar solution in the SS clinic at Harzungen. We also had two-centiliter ampules of Coramine, which was useless for treating edema or dysentery. And thermometers. The thermometers alone created a clinical atmosphere, weaving an unseen web of silence and common cause between the hastily arranged bunks and the medics until darkness began to creep through the windows. But by then everything had been organized, the first two bodies had even been laid along the side wall of the building. When I leaned out the window of my "ward" and saw them, it struck me that at the end of their odyssey they deserved to have their bones covered with sackcloth. Tomorrow someone would commend them to the earth. Aside from the moans and pleas, the building was peaceful and orderly. This couldn't be said of the other quarters, from which we could hear muffled waves of commotion. Only night subdued the struggles for sleeping space and the search for nonexistent food, leaving the air saturated with a distant rumbling. The horizon was a line of rolling murmurs, the sign of our approaching salvation. By day the rumbling receded to some remote corner of the world. Fear still stirred beneath the surface of our endless tasks. We were, after all, in Bergen-Belsen, and though the camp itself was in the background, this was a place of annihilation, and there was no reason for it to single us out for mercy.

One morning a pack of prisoners ignored a sign with skull and crossbones (what was it there for, anyway?) and went looking for water in a brick shed right across from our building—from the hospital. I noticed them as I went to the window to see how long the row of bodies was getting. Two men had just stepped inside the small building, and the rest scattered when they saw a guard approaching. He was a kid still, with a longish face and dark eyes, skinny in his SS uniform. He didn't speak or shout, he just swore under his breath as he released the safety on his rifle and fired at one of the men as he emerged from the shed carrying a jug of water. The prisoner staggered and fell, and water splashed out as the jug hit the ground. The boy fired again, slowly pulling the trigger. Then he fired at the second man, who had dropped his jug and was hopping on one foot. The boy laughed and once more carefully pulled the trigger. I lost sight of the victim as he tried to escape, the corner of the hospital blocking my view. Judging by the boy's smile as he shouldered his rifle—he had enjoyed this—it could have come out either way. Still entertaining, even if the hopper got away. Then the guard began to curse loudly over the body that lay motionless, and I realized he was a Croat *ustaša*. I felt hollow at the sound of kindred Slavic words spoken in such circumstances, but was also surprised at the daring of our striped comrades. The fact that resistance was still alive though it had long seemed dead was to me proof that the world of the crematoria was finished.

But I had some useful work to do just then, because someone had brought in sulfa tablets. Who knows where or how the busy fingers had found them. Most likely in some veterinary station, because the tablets were as big as bottle tops and I had to break them in quarters, and even then a patient would have a hard time swallowing them. But what counted was that I had sulfa and that now the ritual could proceed, both for the patients and for myself. Another question, how they would benefit from it, for sulfa is no nutrient for dehydrated protoplasm. Along the wall outside, the row of bodies grew. Our building was so filled, even the attic was used. I went upstairs to the attic, I don't know why. Perhaps out of zeal to find more patients with dysentery or edema, or else to break the spell of savagery and indecision by doing something different, or simply from the need a captive feels to walk the perimeter of his captivity. It wasn't the kind of attic where secrets are kept, a hodgepodge of objects as ancient as the cobwebs that wreathe them. There were only huge, heavy beams rising up at angles from floor to ceiling. Zebra-striped people lay on the floor beneath the beams, wedged into each other every which way, and the voices in this tangled mass were foul bubbles escaping from mud. The attic window was open. The cold air that came through cleared away some of the stink, but the bodies had formed a semicircle around the window to avoid the cold. Except for one person who lay right in front of it, alone in the piercing air, swept from the solid human shore and now drifting out to the sea of nothingness. Some impatient stretcher bearer had dumped him there. I was disturbed by the shape of his limbs, the peculiar way they sprawled. It was familiar, the shaved head belonged to Ivanček. Then I saw his bright, lively eyes, which were searching for me. As is always the case in the last stages, the remaining moisture of his body had collected in them, glistening, yet they still preserved the timidity of a young boy whose swashbuckling adventure tales had been replaced by inconceivable images of assembly-line death. While his eyes besieged me, as though they were not only trying to escape death's straitjacket but also wanted to communicate to me all the fury of his physical being, I once again saw the kind, pleading smile he had as he left Harzungen. Because precisely at the moment we had to walk to the station, fleeing the pincers of eastern and western fronts, precisely at that moment Ivanček received —who knows how—a package from his village in Slovenia. "Beautiful golden biscuits," he said, holding the parcel in his lap like a young mother awkward with her newborn. It was as though his family had managed to come to their little boy's rescue in the nick of time, had come all the way from the other side of the world. I suppose he brought me his biscuits because I had given him mess tins of stew left over from the day's corpses, in exchange for which he would bring from the tunnels pieces of wood for the stove. He carried the wood under his shirt so the guards wouldn't see it. But this afternoon he had stuffed his shirt with biscuits and tied a ragged apron tightly around his waist, the blue-and-gray stripes billowing as if they covered some animal. He stroked the shapeless hump, protected it with his hands, as if aware of the sanctity of the provisions his native land had sent him for his final, long ordeal. Now, however, he lay on the floor, alone. "Ivan," I tried to rouse him with the confident voice of people who imagine they have firm ground beneath their feet, but it came out lame and hollow, and his eyes were right to repulse it. I didn't look into them when I crouched down beside him and put my ear close to his mouth like a mountain climber listening at the edge of the precipice that swallowed his partner. Words came piecemeal, faint, and told me that it was from the golden biscuits he moistened in his mouth that he had slowly drawn life, every day, day after day, for the duration of our aimless wandering in open cattle cars, where he stood without protection against the hard mass of bodies pressing up against his shirtfront stuffed with rations, or against the hands that grabbed, the knees that shoved, the feet that trampled until they finally trampled his body to the floor. I knelt over his dehydrated head, powerless to help, nor could I have saved him had I known he was lying on the floor of one of those cars that I walked past so many times when we bandaged gangrene cases and carried corpses to the two cars nearest the engine. I wouldn't have had anything to give him—but at least he could have had a quiet corner to himself, like Janoš's Pole. I could have broken off the end of an ampule of fructose and poured the sweet liquid in his mouth. Distressed, I ran for a syringe and the large ampules, as if zeal combined with the right cere-monial objects could turn back the clock. That's what we hope for. We hope that kindness will prevail and lives will be saved. This is the innocent, beautiful instinct of our youth, which sometimes survives our youth and lives on stubbornly. I pulled away the faded, stinking striped outer skin to reveal the boy's plucked, cranelike bones. I had seen thousands of such bones, carried dozens to the anteroom of the oven, but in the presence of this body my professional calm vanished. I had tried to save this life with the food of our dead, and it was now leaving me with the good-natured smile of a Slovene boy. I couldn't find a place for the needle between bone and the coarse, thin skin stretched over it. The sunken thigh was unresponsive, and the sugar water ran out of his mouth. He probably couldn't have been helped even if a doctor had injected plasma into his veins. A sudden anxiety came to his eyes, similar to the irritability of old age, and it didn't subside even after I carried him to the quiet of a dark corner. He probably did not know who was laying him down in a military grain bin side by side with other bodies. I went back downstairs, and as I started splitting the huge sulfa tablets, I thought that soon, that very afternoon, Ivanček would be lying in a row with others beneath my window, and this seemed a lesser evil than my defeat, than my silent shame, than my powerlessness. Without faith, machinelike, I halved the huge tablets meant for good-natured horses and that human bodies would therefore resist.

I have slid down the grassy slope that separates the last terrace from the barbed-wire fence. Here, on a bit of level ground, were once a cesspit and a ditch for ashes. There is a miniature graveyard on this spot now, no more than two bedsheets wide, bordered by simple stones each of which bears an inscription. *Honneur et patrie.* Honor and country. Next to that, *Ossa humiliata.* Humiliated bones. Two phrases in which man has tried to condense the truth of an infinite reality. What fills me with defeat now is not the holy secret of these terraces but the silence in which careful and persistent planners have enshrouded our *ossa humiliata.* Those who swore that they would disinfect Europe completely turned their attention instead to other, less noble interests, interests whose pursuit was in conflict with the demand for denazification. And so instead of undergoing purification Europe emerged from the immediate post-war years an invalid, fitted with glass eyes so it wouldn't frighten good citizens with its empty sockets. The average European accepted this, for Europeans, despite all the high-flown phrases, are basically thoughtless and cowardly. They became accustomed to a comfortable existence. And if now and then they feel shame, they drown it in an orgy of moralizing, in stigmatizing the younger generation, whose legacy of honesty and justice they have already squandered. Today's standardized man may be awakened, who knows, only by some new lay order that dons striped camp burlap and floods the capitals of our countries, unsettling the complacency of shopping malls with the harsh clatter of their wooden clogs. The urns of ashes stored here would have to be taken in processions to all the cities of Germany. Night and day, month after month, men in striped uniforms and wooden clogs would serve as the honor guard beside red earthen pots in the main square of every German metropolis.

Humiliated bones. Though there is a monument forty-five meters tall on the hill above the camp, and a field of cenotaphs dedicated to each Frenchman who died here for his country, this hidden bit of earth is dearer to me. It's more truly ours, remote and hidden, mixing everyone in the same way that their ashes were mixed. Up above, France has erected a cross and tablet for each of her sons, but underneath the splendid rows of white crosses there is nothing—not a fistful of gray dust mingles with the mountain earth. Up there, a national monument, while down here, a sanctuary for all humankind.

I want to say something now to my former companions, but cannot. I am alive, and that fact makes my best thoughts insincere, my best feelings impure. Distracted, I climb back up to the terrace and become part of the crowd listening to the guide. As he speaks, their heads turn slightly toward the steep, grassy slope. He tells them that there was a cesspit down there that collected the sewage from all the terraces, and that sometimes the cesspit would overflow into the ditch of bones and ashes. Whenever the garden up top needed fertilizing, he said, they would send men down here with buckets.

It strikes me that I am hearing many things today for the first time. I slowly make my way to the barracks with the chimney. I would prefer not to have witnesses. Bit by bit I grasp the power that a monument has, even if only a gravestone, to perpetuate a dead person's presence among the living. A pinch of soft ashes does not evoke the right image. And yet I remain a person of fire and ashes, and I am at home on these terraces. When I returned to Trieste after the war, I couldn't understand my father's weekly pilgrimage to the family crypt. The way he would pick flowers to take along. Now that he too is gone, I speak and write about him, but I am reluctant to go to the cemetary where he lies alongside Mother and Marica. My sister occasionally chides me for it, but I can't reacquire the taste for a ritual that I lost on this mountainside, and in Dachau, Dora, and Harzungen. I was present at so many funerals that they would amount to several cemetery visits a day of all the years left me. No, I can't confine the past to a visit of a man's remains, even if they are the remains of my dear father. I have been to the family tomb, but it was only a formality. I experienced nothing.

On the other hand, a while earlier, when I was standing in front of the crude iron elevator that connects the cellar with the oven, Ivo refused to materialize for me. I am too infected with the life I come from. The energy that beats from me repulsed Ivo even before we managed to find words to revive our onetime friendship. Despite my connection to the secrets of this place, I only half exist in its dreamlike, silent atmosphere, and similarly, when I am far from here,

my existence is only half, for half is this atmosphere. The
phoenix hasn't shaken off the ashes from which it rose.

I stop. People are still in the barracks. Children are tum-
bling down the grassy slope that starts behind the cellar and
the elevator as if this were an orchard back home. They
ignore their mother, who has stepped away from the oven
and shakes her finger at them. Meanwhile, with both hands
a little girl grabs one of the cables that anchor the crematorium's slender chimney, and runs around it. Something
above creaks, and I shudder, as if in fear that this witness
to our destruction will be damaged, this sacrificial altar of
Europe—when I should have wished that the child's hands
would pull down the structure of evil.

The people have gone. Without breaking the silence, a new
group has arrived. Because of the regular intervals at which
groups are admitted, it is impossible for a larger crowd to
gather. In these mute shifts the visitors are perpetually re-
plenished delegations from the world of the living. There
are always some ready to set out on a pilgrimage, to visit
graves and shrines, and we think of such people as good,
noble. But there is no evidence that they influence the course
of history. They stand bowed like weeping willows in those
places where endless silence follows devastation. The silence
here is now broken by the words of an elderly tour guide.
He leans on a cane, shifting his weight from foot to foot,
surrounded by a small group. Maybe he's retired and makes

some money on the side doing this, but of course I prefer to think that he is a former resident. For a second, as they enter the barracks, I imagine that I am a spy designated by my invisible comrades to keep an eye on whoever is about to speak in the name of all the silenced tongues. The guide's voice inside the cell block is sober and earnest, he speaks in a way that doesn't repulse me, slowly, without any Ciceronian tricks, making his words fit the images. I have no objections to his presentation. But when he begins to relate the story of the young Alsatian women, I lean against the outside wall of the long barracks, feeling no less weak and fevered than I did at the time. The terraces are still. There is no trace of those women in the sun's rays or on the narrow stairs. They exist only in the cells of my brain, and that isn't enough. As if trying to say something comforting in conclusion, the guide explains that resistance fighters took the camp a short time later *à l'arme blanche,* in hand-to-hand combat, and Radio London announced that event with the phrase *La tortue a gagné la course.* A poetic phrase, the tortoise has won the race. The underground had to make use of code words to keep occupied territory in touch with the free world. But what impression does a phrase like that make on people who have seen the oven and the gently sloping cement floor? The guide should have left the tortoise out of it. Besides, when liberators seized this place, we were already trapped behind other barbed wire.

Two stragglers. A tall young African and a French girl,

both thin. They can't get in because the barracks door is blocked by visitors, so they remain alone on the steps, in a silence that for them has no mysterious presence. His hand restrains her as she stands on the last step, to prevent her from entering. Perhaps, I think, he can't face it. His race, after centuries, can sense the emanations of destruction. But I soon see I am mistaken. A fidgety cheerfulness radiates from his young mouth and eyes. He is bored, he cannot wait to be someplace else, alone with his girl. Now he folds his arm around her waist and they walk to the end of the terrace. He's eager to kiss her again, even though he probably just did, higher up on the steps, as they lagged behind the rest of the group. Over there, at the edge, where the mound drops off to the barbed wire, he will embrace her, and maybe already is embracing her now that I am walking away. And when he does, not only will the double wire fence not bother him, he may not even see it, or for that matter the tall yellow grass, or the guard tower standing like an abandoned pagoda among the mountains. I don't quarrel with him, he moves in a different dimension, one of growth and germination. No, it would be childish, meaningless, to transport these two lovers to our former world. Our apocalypse was in the domain of nothingness, while these two exist in the domain of love, which is just as infinite and which rules just as absolutely and unfathomably over its subjects.

I follow the visitors as they move up the steps. The last is a man with a bad leg, two girls supporting him, presumably his daughters. As he raises the lame foot from one step to the next, he leans on the girls with all his weight. A picture reminiscent of the camp, except that no one helped the cripples back then. The grinding of gravel underfoot also echoes in my memory. The quality of the sound is different, the tread of wooden clogs was harsher, more hollow. As I watch them climb to the highest terrace, suddenly a group of decent Sunday sightseers turns into a shapeless herd. They vanish from sight, and I walk across the meadow I never owned but which was and still is mine. Meadow, I say, because there are no barracks anymore, they've been removed. It is impossible to preserve indefinitely wooden buildings covered with snow in winter, battered by rains in spring, and baked by the sun in summer. Of the fourteen original barracks only four have been preserved—two up above, and two at the bottom. The long, empty spaces have been strewn with gravel, and at the end of each terrace is a low column with the name of one of the camps where Frenchmen were exterminated. Dachau, Mauthausen, Buchenwald, Kochem, Neckagerath, Harzungen. But all the French dead are up there, beyond the barbed wire, united symbolically in their common necropolis.

No visitor will see the living figures behind the name Neckagerath, for instance, or Harzungen. There were so many Frenchmen in Harzungen, they had the final say in running the infirmary, which was of enormous importance in saving lives. By and large we got along well, especially since I didn't take part in the camp's politics. The clinic was small but occasionally required quick and able hands. In the mornings Vaska and I would carry one or two bodies to the bin behind the barracks and throw the mattresses on the ground to let them dry out a little. But the mattresses were usually so soaked that in the evening we would just flip them over for the new patients. On a table by the window was a thermometer, a package of white powder, and a package of pulverized charcoal. Three times a day I shook some of the white powder into a cup and added water to make a soft paste. I went from bunk to bunk, inserting a spoonful of the white mixture between half-opened parched lips and yellow teeth. Some of the patients greedily seized at the paste in an attempt to stanch the life that was steadily seeping out. Others were barely aware of the spoon at their mouths, yet they smacked their lips and swallowed the sticky mess. When they died, they had white cement on their teeth and around their lips. Administering the charcoal was more awkward, as mouths would blow it off the spoon, or cough it out when they tried to swallow. That would be a day of corpses with black teeth and lips. The patients lay still, but would get up, even if they were half-conscious, to keep from voiding on their mattresses. There would be a brown track on the floor behind them. Attending to patients who had tuber-culosis on top of dysentery was even worse. They lay on the eight bunks just left of the entrance and waited for the truck from Dora to come for them. But we never had advance warning when the truck would come, so at the last minute Vaska had to run to the storeroom for their clothes. For their rags. He would bring back the small, filthy bundles and untie them, shouting obscenities as the sweat poured off him. But there was no way we could hurry, since these patients couldn't be dressed in bed, with their bones digging into the mattresses, and they couldn't stand up, either. We would grab them by the legs and under the arms and lay them on the floor. To pull a crumpled trouser leg onto a jutting bone is no simple matter. Vaska would get angry, not at the body on the floor but at its destruction. Meanwhile I would be slipping a striped jacket that looked more like a dust rag under the ribs of another poor devil, grateful to Vaska for being so good to them, even if he did curse. Sweating, we stepped carefully through the bodies lying every which way amid the rubbish. Sometimes we would pull one up to let the bones sit, and then a twiglike hand would reach for the clogs, glassy eyes following its progress. Or for slippers, a wooden spoon, a piece of string. Objects for furnishing your loneliness. One patient who knew it was snowing outside reached for his cap. Vaska got angry again, because the man was unaware that he would die with or without his cap. Still, he looked for it in the infected clutter, and when he found it, he carefully placed the crumpled halo of striped burlap on his bare skull. Vaska became even angrier when Pierre told us to hurry, opening the door a crack and sticking his nose in, apparently without a thought of helping. We stayed crouched on the floor a while more, and finally set a fully dressed skeleton upright. We supported it, one on either side, all the way down the corridor. As it slowly set one foot in front of the other, Vaska would give it a slap on the back, causing the head to bob and the cap to slip on the skull. Finally we got them all onto the truck, and since three bins of corpses had already been loaded, we set our patients on top of the bins, Vaska steadily cursing the driver for honking his horn. The temperatures were near zero, but the bodies lying and sitting on the unfinished wooden lids couldn't feel the cold anymore. The two of us ran back to the barracks, relieved that we had performed our task well.

My attachment to the infirmary was not, however, solely a matter of devotion to work. I had been advised repeatedly not to sleep in the same area as my patients, but I stubbornly stuck by them. Partly out of superstition: staying in the crowded room meant that I was living in the very lair of death, and was thus protected, being too close for it to attack me. But a bond of friendship surely figured in this, too. I lay in the corner, in the lower bunk. Vaska's bunk was over mine. We were the only two hale sailors below decks on this narrow wooden ship with its doomed crew. When Vaska got up in the morning and scrambled out of his bunk, and I followed, I felt like a captain who had remained loyal to his crew, even though my first task of the day would be to commend some of them to the sea's bottomless depths. Then, too, maybe there is a streak of Slavic fatalism in me. Maybe

I thought that Vaska and I couldn't expose ourselves to infection any more than when we pulled the rotting rags back onto the dying. Though they say a person is most vulnerable when he sleeps. But caution in the world of crematoria could just as well expose one to danger as keep one from it.

This morning there was a disturbing wetness in my mouth, like too much saliva. Vaska hadn't got up yet. I assumed it was still early, or he would have been fidgeting over my head, since it was his job, along with other aides, to scrub down the corridors of both barracks before daylight. I swallowed and listened to the gurgling in the chest of the patient two bunks to the right of me. He'll be dead within a day, I thought, and swallowed again. Suddenly alarmed at swallowing so much fluid, I sat bolt upright. A cold shudder went through me. It was as though silver had burst inside my skull and in the darkness before my eyes—a flash that revealed the world in its entirety, both living and doomed. I got up and quickly walked between the bunks out of the room. I ran, although it was clear I couldn't escape from myself. I wanted fresh air, but found myself in the narrow washroom, which was quiet in the dim, gray predawn light. In the middle of the room, water dripped slowly from the showerheads. The stove was right at hand. Everything was as it always was, except that now for the first time I realized I was surrounded. My head twitched. Hesitantly I went to the window. The barbed wire outside was no longer the plait of knots I had always gazed at without seeing, it had become a visible, tangible sign of my captivity. This was the lucidity of a condemned man, before the darkness closes in. At that moment I was aware that the handkerchief I held to my mouth was the only object I still had from home. Soaked with my blood. My head twitched again. And then the slow, steady drops falling onto the cement calmed me. The rhythmic sound evoked images of the work details returning toward evening, the hot water rinsing the diarrhea off their parchmentlike hips and thighs. I could see myself leading them afterward down into the narrow room, and for a second it struck me that the time had come to make arrangements for my gravedigger's duties. The thought of my work calmed me, and I returned to my bunk. But I went back mainly because I had just swallowed again, and this time only saliva. Vaska got up soon and jumped past me to the floor. This was the familiar sequence of events. I tried to still my fears, to harden myself. After such a shock it isn't easy to do this, but one has to pretend that nothing has damaged one's blind-and-deaf faith in self-preservation.

Harzungen! The name is inscribed on the smooth surface of the short pillar before me. What meaning can it have for these tourists? Unless you were to bring in one of the work shifts that left the camp three times a day for the tunnel, and have these Sunday visitors go with them. If Jupp hadn't asked me to stand in for him, even I would never have known what all the weak and wounded returned from each evening.

"I have diarrhea," Jupp said as he handed me a little wooden medicine kit with a leather handle. He was a long and lanky Dutchman, but I didn't realize how long and lanky until he bent down and deposited the box on the floor beside the table. That night I left the camp in his place. The snow shone metallic in the dark. As I walked, I was overcome by a wave of uncertainty and desperate nostalgia for my little nook in death's antechamber. But then I was distracted by the marching of our formations, which for a while appeared like rows of real workers. But when we came within earshot of the shouting and the searchlights, that illusion vanished. The men had stuffed the bottoms of their jackets, which were as flimsy as kitchen aprons, into their trousers so they wouldn't flap in the icy, eight-degree wind; clogs thudded dully against the snow's crust; hands were tucked in pockets and shoulders hunched, as though that would provide protection for the jutting ears and the shaven heads in buckram caps. Not just the head, the whole body longed to fold into a tiny ball. At the front of the column a shriek would pierce the cold air, and be repeated like the caws of countless crazed ravens. It was the Germans, our hidden shepherds, shouting to draw a fence of fear around the herd as it hobbled and tripped in the north wind. But I wasn't too cold, I had my brown coat. It reached down only to my knees but was heavy and in good condition. A square had been cut out on the back and then mended with the striped camp material. The cold would have had no trouble penetrating my trousers, except that I had on two layers of long underwear, including a pair that Vaska and I had pulled off an old Frenchman before we carried him to the bin. God knows how the man came by the pair. He had a warm undershirt, too. Vaska put them in a jug of water and let them boil for a while. And so the corpses not only fed me, they clothed me, too, because I gave them charcoal and carried them out of the barracks.

On that night journey I brought along Jupp's medicine kit with a red cross on the side, but the bodies hopping through the dark, as if the cold were a shower you could duck, had little use for bandages and aspirin. The lines stopped on a railway embankment, swarmed over the tracks, and began stomping in their clogs. Six hundred pairs of clogs. Flashlight beams darted up and down the striped mass until a train of four cars arrived and we attacked it to escape the cold, the shouting, the poisoned night. The cars rattled, and the bodies puffed in the dark in an attempt to warm this icebox whose windows had been boarded over. I stood in the corridor and clutched the medicine kit between my knees so the crowd wouldn't trample it. The desperate jostling made twenty minutes pass like a flash. The convoy stopped and was surrounded again with beams of light and shouts. They lashed those of us who jumped into the snow and those who fell into it because they were too weak to jump, in their effort to join the formation already in place. It was almost consoling to hear close by the hollow sound of a stream melting the snow's crust, followed by the smell of warm urine. The shouts got the gray detachment going. It tramped through Niedersachs-werfen and past the houses as if through a distant memory of snow-covered homes where the human race, now extinct, once enjoyed winter and sitting around a crackling fire. The procession stopped in front of a long line of steel carts. Bodies climbed up, levering themselves with arms and legs, and for a moment remained suspended over the steel edge before finally sliding inside the huge, Krupp-manufactured carts, the kind that miners fill with ore. Then night swallowed the last flashlight beams, and the steel boxes jolted, grated, and started rolling. As at a signal, snow began to fall. The small engine gave off puffs of warm steam, and arms and legs longed to reach that skybound warmth. The convoy darted snakelike through the night, while our wooden soles pounded the floor as if to break the steel shell of fate. The dark mass clustered in the center, away from the icy sides, backs and bellies pressing together, heads retracting turtle-like, chins hugging chests.

The sad howl of a siren ended this long journey. Brakes squealed, and figures with machine guns jumped out, a pack of barking wolves attacking a column of sleighs. Then the night's silence appeared to calm them, and they began to stomp their feet in the snow, though they had boots and fur caps and fur-lined overcoats reaching practically to the ground and on top of that camouflaged canvas capes. Mean-while the engines of a thousand planes filled the sky, a friendly sound, but so distant and dreamlike that the bodies with death in their bones hardly noticed it. The clattering of the clogs stopped. There was a stench of diarrhea, and the human cargo cursed and moved to force the offender from its midst. The guards were startled, nervous that any commotion might draw the planes' attention. A lone figure now stood against the steel side, apart from the rest. The silence didn't last long. A squad appeared, leading German shepherds that for no reason threw themselves on the huge carts, barking wildly and making as if to bite through the steel. Then the sound of the planes and the dogs was gone, leaving only the stomping of clogs against the steel bottoms of the carts, the rhythm of our misery.

Another time, a day departure, I was standing in for Jan, who like Jupp was tall and skinny, a ship's mast of a man. But he was less talkative than Jupp, and judging by his look, he probably hadn't treated the natives that well in the Dutch East Indies, where he bragged of having been. He wasn't sick, either, when he asked me to take his place. He just couldn't bring himself to go out in the bitter cold. But I agreed to go—for the experience. It gave me a sense of purpose. I would be with bodies that moved. For eight hours I would not be a witness to limbs melding with mattresses. And perhaps also I wished to touch the world outside the barbed wire, or else to let the outside world touch me. Except that that world was just as poisoned as ours. As we returned through Niedersachswerfen in the afternoon, our ranks could barely move their swollen feet. Four men carried an unconscious body, one limb on each bended shoulder and the torso hanging low in the middle like a gigantic spider. Two young girls walked out onto the white and quiet winter street without casting a glance at the column as it hobbled past. Two young girls ignoring a parade of six hundred zebra-striped prisoners. They walked down the sidewalk, enjoying the snow on a pleasant sunny day. A small dairy, a watchmaker's shop, a barbershop, and a bakery stood empty.

Our shift leader was Peter, who although he had a green triangle sewn onto his uniform under his number, as did all German criminals, did not mistreat the workers. They said he held up a bank or embezzled money, but his relationship to us was earnest and well-intentioned. He never hurried the crowd as it gathered before leaving camp, people jostling to get near me so I could excuse them from work. "Me! Me!" they called in every language. "Look at me! Look at me!" One forced his way forward, unbuttoning his trousers until they slipped to his ankles. His withered thighs looked as if they were covered with coffee grounds, as did his scaly calves. I gave him a hospital pass, certain that I would see him in my ward by evening. Then I filled out a pass for a man with fleshy hooves instead of feet; he forced his way past several prisoners who were struggling not to fall amid the surge of bodies and voices. I stuck a thermometer under one person's arm while I filled out a pass for another, and another. A choppy sea assailing me from all sides. "Look at me! Look at me!" This went on until the front door opened and Kapo

Peter got us marching in place. *"Links, zwo, drei, vier. Links, zwo, drei, vier."* Outside the guardhouse an officer counted us. He strutted around like a stiff rooster. I approached him with my wooden medicine kit, pleased as a lawyer is pleased when he's just proven the innocence of his client, and handed him the fifteen passes, an attempt to outwit death. One could argue that this attempt was irrelevant, since my passes delayed death only by a day or two. Who knows, though, maybe one or two people would survive. Even that small hope is worth an entire life's work.

A pale sun shone over the trampled snow. Two houses stood by the roadside. Not a soul anywhere, except for a small child, probably standing on a footstool, his face pressed against a window pane. He smiled as if watching a parade of circus clowns, his smile as out of place and time as the sun above. Someone lit a brownish cigarette butt and offered it to me. In the mingling of European languages and in the snow, the Russian steppe joined with the French plains and the Dutch lowlands to create an illuminated image of salvation. This image was even more vivid as we walked through Niedersachswerfen, with Ukrainian families hitching their horses to big sleighs outside their wooden barracks and children sledding down the hillsides. Add to it our hobbling procession, our rags and clogs, and you have a Brueghel winter scene. The ranks then began to fill up the Krupp carts, elbows latching onto edges and legs searching for support. A woman at the window of a house across the way watched. She didn't wipe her eyes like the Alsatian women in Markirch. The look in her face was surprised, almost bewildered, as though she couldn't comprehend the reality of so many ruined males.

The sun hadn't set and the cold was bearable. Several guards sat on a wooden cart between the rows of steel bins. Unlike an ordinary flat cart, this one had a trapezoid-shaped arch running down the middle, forming a narrow space with two ledges on which the SS men could sit and rest their feet. Their rifles wedged between their legs, they ground the snow with their feet and stared ahead like hunters with no imagination. This is how the pair would sit in the barracks when the shift left for the tunnels. Perched on a bench near the stove, they watched as I bandaged the wound of a returnee. They would be bored, of course, but it was better to huddle by the fire of smooth briquettes than to stand for eight hours in the drafts of the tunnels with compressors roaring and explosions going off. Once or twice the Kapo stopped in to chat, but not for long, and left them to stare out the window at the network of small-gauge tracks that covered the plain and eventually vanished into the tunnels. Only at the sound of a major detonation would they flinch, barely raising their backsides off the bench. The camp siren wailed frequently. I went on bandaging a gangrenous limb, and then the hand of a fellow who was covered with dust, as if he had come out of a flour mill. The fingers of his right hand were missing the knuckles. He sharpened the bit for the compressor, he explained, holding the hand outstretched as though it wasn't his. He even smiled, because the hand was so cold it didn't hurt, and he was grateful for the wound, which brought him into the warmth of the barracks. The dysentery cases sat in the corner, stunned by exertion, hunger, and the warm air that smelled of urine.

When Peter flew into a fury because of a German engineer, things grew lively for a while. The engineer was young and fair-haired and wore a leather jacket. He burst into the barracks like a whirlwind and began strutting in front of the patients sitting on the bench. One of them had gangrene, another had feet like two heads of cabbage, and a third was caked with excrement. But the engineer shrieked that they were all fakers and slackers and they had better get moving. "Outside, on the double!" he shouted. Instead of looking at him, they turned to me, their orderly, and stayed quietly seated. I told the engineer that I couldn't assume responsibility for the prisoners and that he should talk to Kapo Peter. Then I took a paper bandage, knelt down before a patient sitting on the bench with his trouser leg rolled up, and started to dress his wound. The engineer stormed off, slamming the door behind him, and for a moment I felt as though I were in a mountain lodge enveloped in snow and alpinists were congratulating me for a bold rescue. I had used the word responsibility, as though someone was responsible for what happened to these shattered bodies. It was a word tyrants would have to reckon with to the end of their days. Even the SS men sensed the change in the air; their faces seemed to be coming apart in the warmth, as their power was coming apart. When Peter came back and reprimanded them, the two stared at him pleadingly goggle-eyed. *"Er hat hier nicht verloren!"* Peter yelled, his black hair covering his square forehead, his heavyset legs stomping in the middle of the barracks floor. "Let him come here when I'm here," he shouted, "and I'll show him the way out." An incident so unusual as to be almost dreamlike. I began to think that my medic's calling made some sense.

But before long new guards, a new medic, and a new Kapo arrived, and they made even the sick scramble into the Krupp-made carts. One prisoner had a broken leg and possibly some other fracture, and he lost consciousness. We carried him and placed him on the floor of the wooden cart, and I sat on the snow-covered seat and held onto his good leg to prevent him from sliding off. He lay on the thin crust of ice, unable to feel death seeping through the thin burlap and into his limbs. The following night, a man fell off a high scaffold in the tunnel and was brought into the barracks soft and practically invertebrate; he was transported to Dora because there was no crematorium in Harzungen. No one now for me to look after, but I took my place on the wooden cart anyway, partly so I wouldn't have to climb into one of the steel boxes, but mainly because that night the wooden cart was attached directly to the engine. I sat next to the SS man and turned my shoulders in the wind, exposing first my back to the cold, then my chest. The engine had been reversed, so that its cylindrical smokestack was quite close. A tiny engine for a tiny train. But a smokestack is a smoke-stack, I thought and stood up. I set the box with its red cross against the dark machine's iron surface and stepped onto it. Cautiously gripping the iron, I climbed slowly, because the engine lurched like a horse shying away from a stranger trying to saddle it. Then I worked my way past the cab and threw my arms around the smokestack. The smoke, escaping in heavy puffs, fell onto the long chain of carts and abetted the night in concealing the human shame. I could feel the warmth of the steel like the belly of an animal. The end of humankind, I thought, because all that's left is the compas-sion of hot metal.

Before long the earth started to show black between patches of snow. Every morning several men trundled a rough-hewn tub full of shit out to a field beyond the barbed wire. Their clogs were wrapped in burlap so they could tread through the mud without sinking in. From time to time the brown contents of the tub would spatter their zebra-striped trousers, but you could see that they relished their work all the same. As I stood by the window watching them, I thought I saw a certain recklessness in their movements, or perhaps a cyn-ical self-assurance, as if mocking the bouncing tub whose extraordinary story they knew firsthand. The stench must have been terrible, because the guards kept an eye on them only from a distance.

Though the truck continued to haul bones up to Dora, the mood had changed with the appearance of the planes. At first we were frightened. The bombs they dropped on the other side of the mountain shook the earth and made our barracks creak like superannuated wooden boats. Then machine guns sputtered over the SS mess hall outside the camp. A new tension gathered in our hearts. It seemed a miracle that somewhere on the other side of the world were people who knew about our forlorn outpost, who even knew the location of the guardhouse. The agitated April air brought us new problems. The bombs took down electric lines, leaving the barracks without light that evening, and the water lines too were broken. In the dark our medical-funeral rites became even more grim, particularly in the room for tuberculars. But worse was the lack of water. It was impossible to wash bodies filthy from the waist down, but we still had to put them on mattresses. We worked by the light of a carbide lamp. Nighttime returnees from the tunnels would bring us carbide in exchange for a leftover portion of that day's stew. Vaska had become an inexhaustible gravedigger, tending to the corpses by himself since I moved to the two rooms for communicable diseases. One was used for observation; in the other we had only four beds, one double-tiered bunk on each side. And two patients. An old Belgian lay on the upper bunk against the wall, and a German Gypsy on the lower bunk by the window. The Belgian was dying. The Gypsy sat on his bunk all day and fussed. He was stocky and had a thick head, but it was impossible to make out his features, his face was so distorted with swelling. The eyelids were two yellow snails, and piglike nostrils gaped beneath a flat nose. He had stolen a piece of bread from the Belgian, and as punishment I withheld his portion of stew. I said if he promised not to steal anymore, I would give him his ration, but he refused. "Go ahead and eat my stew," he said as the yellow snails tried to crawl out of his eyes. What was I to do? I couldn't really blame him for creeping up to the Belgian's bunk and taking the bread. That old body had reached the end, anyway. Finally we made up when I promised to get him a cigarette if he stopped stealing. He solemnly swore he would stop, and to make sure he got his cigarette he offered to read my palm. "My hand is fine. Don't worry, you'll get your smoke as long as you don't steal," I told him. "As for the future, who knows what it will bring." I was already some distance from the bunk when he said, "You'll make it home." I didn't object. Of course, that was what we all hoped, although we didn't admit it, observing the tacit rule against tempting death with words of life. But I asked how my wife was doing back home. He twisted his face, exposing the black hairs in his nostrils. "You aren't married," he hissed. "But the one you loved is no longer alive." Clearly, his powers were formidable. I gave him the cigarette. The

Gypsy sat on his mattress like a short tree trunk and inhaled, and gradually the smoke concealed his blistery eyes.

The adjoining room had eight beds—four two-tiered bunks. Both rooms were small, the smallest in the infirmary, but at least there was no smell of festering wounds there. They were for undiagnosed cases. Strange, inexplicable fevers. Now and then there was a dignitary among the patients. The public prosecutor from Antwerp, for one, whose countrymen tried to save him that way. He was getting on in years, was quiet and friendly, but occasionally you could hear the echo of stern authority in his voice. Such people are accustomed to obedience; they expect it even of death. This is also where Jupp slept; he was far too thin for his lungs to support his long body, and that was probably the reason for his fever. And there were two Frenchmen about whom I knew little, Marcel's protegés. Marcel's colleague, Philip, was the one who looked after them. I hoped that the same patronage system would allow me to keep Darko in the room. It wasn't because of any machinations of mine that they had assigned him to my room, but since he was already there, I assumed it would be possible for him to stay. This is how I learned that Marcel was not a good man.

Darko was a Slovene, sixteen years old. Frail as a birch. A high fever in the morning, but none, or even a subnormal temperature, at night. Who knows what was simmering inside his ribcage. He was perpetually good-natured. He sat on the upper bunk in an undershirt and chatted as if he were sitting on the ledge of a tall ceramic stove in a farmhouse near Tolmin. "It was warm there, too," he said, when the order came to evacuate the camp.

At the sound of Russian artillery, approaching from the east, presumably, they had to run into the snow in their shirts. In shirts and clogs, and wrapped in blankets they pulled off their bunks. But running is clumsy when you're wrapped in a blanket, especially through snow. The blanket flaps and catches between your ankles, but if you leave them exposed, your legs will freeze. We all had to run; no choice, because the SS shot those who fell and couldn't go on. And so we kept running till nightfall. They locked us up in a stable for the night, with nothing to eat or drink. We had to leave before dawn, and those who couldn't move the SS finished with a pistol shot to the head. We ran a second day, and a third, before we reached a train. God knows how many days we traveled in the open cars, exposed to the snow. Fortunately Darko kept his blanket with him, otherwise he would have frozen. He kept telling me how cold he was— he hardly mentioned hunger—and as he talked he smiled innocently. I was afraid he'd gone mad. It wouldn't have surprised me if he had. Perhaps he wasn't smiling at me but at the memory of the warmth that enfolded the room back then, because besides charcoal briquettes we used real wood that the day shift brought back from the tunnels at evening. They hid it in their trousers, around the waist. They would unfasten their trousers and place the dirty chunks of wood on the floor, watching with questioning eyes to see if this would win them a mess tin of the day's broth. I would have gladly ladled out a portion for everyone, even without the firewood, but they allotted us very little food because the mortality rate in those two rooms wasn't high, and not much was left over.

One evening a friendly Italian brought in some firewood. He set the dusty pieces of wood on the floor, and when I poured stew into his round, red mess tin, he grasped the bowl both greedily and lovingly. After he ate, he looked at me earnestly and pulled a folded newspaper out of his shirt front. "Here, take this, if you like," he said. It was the official paper of the Italian workers in Germany. Faith in ultimate victory, Mussolini's social republic, the usual propaganda. Paper for kindling a fire. But the rustling of newsprint after so many months released a wave of warmth and light in me. The headlines contained the names of Italian cities which suddenly presented themselves to me in all their splendor, medieval vaults and Gothic arches, the romanesque portals, the frescoes by Giotto, the mosaics of Ravenna. From behind the printed letters, rose windows appeared like distant shore lights through fog. From page three the face of a young film actress looked at me. It didn't exactly match my memory of her; it was more mature, less carefree. Because of the poor-quality paper the features were smudgy, fuzzy, and in the poor light of the carbide lamp they became the features of the woman I had loved. Suddenly, unexpectedly I saw her simple smile, her deep eyes. Her love of good books. Her piano playing. And I desperately wanted her to be alive, to be waiting for me to return like Odysseus from hell. At the same time I was keenly aware that she had preceded me to a place from which there was no return, and that the merciless exterminator was lying in wait for me behind the bunks. I dismissed her image and forced myself to listen to the thick-headed Gypsy snoring on the other side of the door. But the actress's face had been on the front page of a women's illustrated weekly my sister subscribed to, so my sister's bedroom appeared to me, a ray of sunlight gilding the edge of her sewing table and the basket sitting on it. I saw my sister's face, her features as finely sculpted as those of the actress. I cut the picture out of the newspaper the next day and borrowed a jar of paste from a clerk so I could glue it to a piece of cardboard. As a truck driver pastes a bathing beauty to the wall of his cab, or a soldier pins a photograph inside his tent, I set the cardboard portrait on the stool beside my corner bunk. I've never done anything like this before or since.

The staff doctor was unusually chatty that morning, and it seemed he would finish his rounds as quickly as ever. He was tall, muscular, and fair-haired, like a rugby player on the cover of a sports magazine. He approached in the company of Marcel and Philip. The bedsheets had been straightened and tucked under, making death tidy under the smooth blue-and-white checkered material, in accordance with the head physician's will. When the old Belgian's case came up, Marcel said, "*Gestorben,*" and the head doctor inclined his head confidentially, as if among colleagues, to confirm that indeed the old Belgian was going, with gangrene and a host of other problems besides. "*Selbstverständlich,*" Philip concurred. It was revolting to watch them. When they stopped beside Darko's bed, the doctor's large body grew animated. In a raised, self-important voice he again described the high fever of the mornings and below-normal temperatures at night. "*Ja, klar!*" he proclaimed. "*Ja, klar!*" Philip replied fervently. "*Klar! Klar!*" the two repeated. Overwhelmed by his own competence, and wanting to demonstrate it further to his colleagues, the doctor suggested they examine Darko. What extraordinary generosity. Darko glanced around hesitantly; he wasn't sure whether their comments boded well or ill. His childlike face contrasted with his grownup eyes. A few seconds later he was standing in front of them in his undershirt, and his slender, well-defined backside was a bit of freshness among the disintegrating bodies. The doctor struck a pose and bent toward Darko's shoulders. His stethoscope had scarcely brushed the boy's skin before his voice thundered again, "*Klar! Es ist vollständig klar!*" Uncomfortable in the presence of this inspection team, Darko smiled vaguely. Marcel approached him, and of course he too had to exclaim, "*Klar!*" Darko was scrambling back up into his bunk when the doctor said he would send him to Dora. "If you say so," Marcel agreed, hesitating only a little, because he knew Darko was my compatriot. "There are four empty beds," I said. "There's no shortage of space. He can stay here." But the head doctor just waved his beefy hand. "*Nein, nein!* He'll be better off in Dora. They have a special ward there for patients like him." Marcel said nothing, then changed the subject. As I climbed up to Darko's bunk to arrange his sheet, the two clowns kept talking, outdoing each other. Suddenly the head doctor asked, "His wife?," and then whispered something in Philip's ear. Philip giggled. They were referring to the face mounted on the cardboard in my corner. It was all so pathetic, the way they smirked at my helplessness to save Darko, the way Philip flattered his master. The worst part wasn't the tittering behind my back but the obvious fact that this was part of the game they'd played with me and Darko. It would have been futile to oppose the head doctor, to say that Darko was my countryman, to ask that he stay a few more days, and then we would decide. But I should have tried. As it was, I had relied on Marcel. If I had talked with him beforehand, it might have been different, but who could have known they would release Darko and not the Antwerp prosecutor, Jupp, or the two Frenchmen? No, I had only myself to blame, spending all my time with the patients and none with the people in charge. I didn't like to promote myself. I had no ambition, no self-confidence, no thought of acting according to the rules of personal gain. Now I realize that you can do a great deal more for your fellow man if you command authority and respect. Darko would have stayed if Marcel had not been able to go over my head. At least I dressed him properly, so he wouldn't freeze as he sat in the truck on top of a crate. I also gave him a note for Stane; otherwise no one would look after him in Dora amid a sea of patients. As he sat in the truck, Darko smiled a faint smile, as if he knew what was in the crate beneath him; but for my benefit he tried to stay cheerful, even brave.

I resolved I would be a completely different kind of medic. But every thought of the future withered in that world of ultimate negation. My fear of the end—the fear that clouded my inner life at the close of the First World War and as I witnessed the fascist conflagrations—had found its ultimate realization. Srečko Kosovel, the Slovene poet, expressed the essence of that great anxiety, but he wasn't the only one. Ionesco speaks of the same sense of catastrophe. Each individual escapes the fear in his own way. Some with art, others with belligerence. I tried to think it away, that is, I suppressed it. Then in the world of crematoria, where the worst came to pass, I avoided it with work. I automatically renounced all thoughts of the future and memories of the past, parceling myself out in a schedule of daily, hourly actions. I saved myself through concern for others. And just as any thought of my own future was excluded from that concern, so was any thought of the future in general excluded. I lived from moment to moment among the ovens, as dispassionate as a whirring movie camera.

But some thought away the present by living in the past. Željko was a case in point, forever resorting to a fairy-tale concept of love which he kept reviving, elaborating, and deepening. At least he knew how to tell a story. Even his figure hinted at loquaciousness—lanky like a Dutchman, but more agile and more agitated, with a thin, sunburnt face and dark hair. A true Dinaric type. Not in the least arrogant, though, just a shade superior, as his Dalmatian blood dictated. This showed itself as early as our train transport from Dachau to Dora. There were ten of us, ten newly certified medics traveling in a regular train. We sat with other passengers in a spacious section of the car, among them a blonde girl who wasn't afraid of our SS escort. She joked with us. She told me that we looked as if we were wearing pajamas. I smiled, being polite. Željko stood up and forced his way over to me. He wanted me to give him my seat, persisted, but when he saw it wasn't going to happen, he made his way among the knees back to his seat. "He doesn't know how to do it," he grumbled, shrugging his shoulders, while the girl smiled and the SS sitting with us smiled too, like ordinary people.

Željko's supremacy in matters of love was obvious. He would come to see me in the evening, when I was in the room with the dysentery cases. He wore his striped jacket, but instead of the striped trousers he had on dark-blue sweat pants with tight, elasticized cuffs that made his legs seem even longer. "Every girl in Split knows these legs," he would say with a serious look on his pointed face. His nostrils flared, and he was off into the past again, roaming the narrow streets and piers of Split. Or climbing a rocky prominence like a fisherman keeping watch for tuna. He had to be alone when he was out of sorts. As he was sitting on his peak, he caught sight of two young bodies tanning on the strip of sand below. An incomparable vision: steep cliffs rising above the glitter of a sapphire sea, and the chocolate curves of the women lying nymphlike on a sandy haven. Unable to control himself, he threw a stone in a wide arc and it splashed into the water right by the shore. The nymphs started and ran away down the wild beach.

They were all his, the beautiful women, but he didn't know the address of a single one. When he was depressed he would sit in a wicker chair outside a café. None of the women could beguile him, except for one, who pleaded with him for so long that he finally got up and left with her.

But when the Italians occupied Dalmatia, times changed. The jails proved too small for all the young Dalmatian men. The women sent him messages there. "Have they beaten you badly, Željko mine?" How did they manage to hide pieces of paper in the folds of the laundry? When they were no longer allowed to visit him, they sent their little sisters, who would recite the message syllable by syllable, as they had been coached, "Have—they—beat—en—you—bad—ly—Želj—ko—mine?" Some time later there was a big trial in Split, with virtually all the local young people, male and female, sitting in the defendant's dock. The judges questioned them, but the women didn't answer, they just giggled. Then they were all put on a ship, and when the time came to weigh anchor, all of Split turned out on the pier with the very best food that was left in the city. From the deck the young people sang partisan songs. They sang them all the way to Venice, where they were disembarked. Bystanders stared at the tall blondes they had been told were bandits but who were in fact the most beautiful women in Dalmatia. The jails filled with them. Željko was lucky to have a window overlooking a *calle,* as the Venetians call their narrow streets. He had great good luck, because through his heavy bars, in a window right across, he could watch a small young brunette brush her hair. And as she brushed her hair, she would look at him knowingly, and as time went on, she would uncover her breasts for him. She began to send him messages through the warder, she even came to visit, because a woman in love can overcome all obstacles. She wept when they were moved to southern Italy. There, too, people took them for bandits at first, but later the air-raid alarms became more frequent and the locals sought shelter under the roof of the prison. And the women came during the alert to chat with the prisoners through their grated windows.

Željko sat on the edge of my bunk, his pole-like legs

stretched across the floor. His storytelling transported him and me out of our closed circle. Yes, he escaped through the spell of love, drawing his confidence from its light. I, on the other hand, felt trapped, stifled. The difference between us became striking when the time came to evacuate from the camp. The order was that all able bodies leave first thing in the morning. But Željko, a medic, could stay with his patients. Marcel tried to persuade him to stay, but he wouldn't. I had thought that our bond of friendship would keep him here. Hadn't we spent all our free time together? That morning, because of the discharge from my lungs, it was difficult for me to walk; I often had to lie down. But Željko couldn't wait to go off in pursuit of his shining vision. "If they have to, they'll bomb the barracks and all the rotting bodies in them," he argued. Perhaps, but I had to stay with my invalids. Perhaps I felt that I would be safe only if I remained part of the infirmary, that working for the common good would make me less vulnerable if not immune. But immunity was an illusion. My own infection was proof of that. And Mladen's death.

Marcel couldn't determine with his stethoscope which side, right or left, was affected. He told me he could hear nothing, and sent me to the radiologist in Dora. I found myself traveling alongside the crates that Vaska and I had filled and that several times had made the infirmary Kapo lose his temper. It didn't suit his German sense of precision to have the yellow soles of a corpse's feet sticking out from under the lid. But the two of us couldn't help it that some bodies were longer than others. And with three corpses to a crate, there was no way the lid would sit neatly. This Kapo had been in the camp for eleven years and had good reason to be peevish, because he was a Communist. He hated checking teeth before each body went into the crate. The two of us would set the stretcher down on the ground behind the barracks, and he would inspect the wide-open jaws. He was sullen every time he pulled a tooth for Hitler's gold reserves, which was why he grumbled at Vaska and me. For he was a likable person, with a long, intelligent face. He would often amuse himself with a fourteen-year-old Russian boy who lay in Janoš's big room because of a wound in his leg that had long since healed. It occurred to me that it probably wouldn't take eleven years for the prospect of cavorting with those rosy-pink limbs to start appealing to me. The Kapo also drank rubbing alcohol sometimes and stumbled around the barracks like a shadow.

So Marcel sent me to Dora and I agreed, mainly to see Stane and Zdravko, though I asked myself why I deserved having my chest x-rayed when bodies lay in crates that jumped to the truck's periodic jolts. What right did I have to contemplate them as if from the far shore of a wide river? A few kind impulses weren't enough to redeem me in the face of millions of dead. How did I become a medic? The Slovene at Dachau who added my name to the list of new medics was trying to save someone who he thought might be useful to his people. I don't know who he was, but since then I have tried to do everything in my power not to disappoint him. And, if he is no longer living, not to dishonor his ashes. But on that ride I felt guilty. The canvas fluttered, and the SS man behind me cursed the driver for the jolts.

Why, I wondered, was this man allowed to live? Because he was a good executioner? But he probably wasn't. Just dullwitted, like the vast majority of human beings. A mouth that chewed, a stomach that digested, genitals that worked like a piston in a motor. He cursed because he kept losing his balance as the truck turned corners, but if he had come to his senses while there was still time, he wouldn't now be guarding skeletons in a truck speeding to the city of death. But his mind had been numbed, just as his homeland was submerged in night.

That night, I lay on the floor with rows of consumptives, waiting for a radiologist in full battle gear, with rubber gloves and a leather shield in front of him. At the far end of the barracks, at the end of the corridor, was the room in which he examined ribcages, while on the hill outside, a huge mound of bodies burned. He didn't tell me what he found, but he dismissed me in five minutes.

I had to wait several days for a truck to take me back to Harzungen. That was at the height of the great resettlements from the East, and Dora was filled with trucks coming from the train station. Otherwise everything was the same as in December. The barracks were scattered in ravines or on outcroppings, resembling mountain cabins. But on the level ground below they were neatly arrayed, camp-style. Through the middle ran a wide road, wider than the one in Dachau, leading to an imposing gate, and beyond, giving one a sense of limitless distance. At the entrance stood a guard, as though at the approach to a drawbridge. Formations of prisoners marched past in the morning and again at night. As I watched them from my barracks atop the hill, they looked dreamlike: rows of infantry moving along a level road, the gray-and-blue stripes of their clothing lending them a special, broken rhythm. In the morning and at night music played at the entrance for this procession. Inspirational marches in the morning, and at night, marches honoring labor. As the columns moved like a river of blue-and-gray mud, a squadron of lost souls blew on their instruments at the cemetery gate. The musicians had every right to use their profession to save their lives and get an extra helping of food. But this was a bitter sort of playing, full of shrill notes.

All day long the trucks brought in stacks of skeletons that would be powdered with fine snow, like lime. A truck would stop on the slope, the military driver would step down, careful not to get into the ruts, and light a cigarette. Meanwhile men in zebra stripes would handle the load. They wore black rubber gloves up to the elbows. One would step into the truck to yank a body off the heap in the corner and pull it outside. He moved quickly, because the next truck would be rumbling in soon. The snow-sprinkled bodies almost seemed to come to life, slipping from his arms and sliding to the ground, as if to simplify his work for him. The rubber gloves threw them onto a pile, and there were bearers with wooden stretchers that had taut wire nets. The driver hurried them because he would have to go any minute now. Two bearers set a stretcher on the ground and lay a desiccated thing on it, whose ribs were like the wicker of a mason's basket, a thing that had recently stood upright like them and had been dressed in the same striped rags as theirs. They'd long since grown accustomed to their work and weren't the slightest bit disconcerted. They were like young construction workers, smirking at a joke as they piled bricks onto a hand-barrow, or like woodsmen carrying their logs to the charcoal makers at the top of a hill and carefully stepping across slippery clay, or like smugglers sneaking their goods over a border—except that this cargo had no value, it was as abundant as weeds, and the true border was the line between life and nothingness that what they carried had crossed long ago.

In the midst of this peaceful scene we were engaged in a conversation about Dora. Zdravko told me that originally the camp was a hillside and that a group of men in stripes were brought here, given picks and shovels, and told to dig ditches big enough for shelter and sleeping. Then the ditches were expanded into mines, and because the work couldn't wait, half the workers slept while the other half set off explosives, and new workers came, and in this way were made the tunnels that housed the V-1 and V-2 rockets that flew across the English Channel and brought death to English cities. Besides the German engineers and mechanics there were all sorts of capable specialists in zebra stripes who were forced to help, among them brilliant individuals, especially French and Russian. The French supposedly even had their own radio transmitter; at any rate the SS once searched for something so feverishly that they ripped all the straw from their mattresses. The Russian and French technicians who worked on the airborne bombs sabotaged their complex and sensitive mechanisms. The Russian mechanics were said to have urinated into the tubing, so that when transported to France and set up on their launch pads, the bombs would not work. Another time, paper was stuffed into the pipes. The bombs had to be brought back again, a whole train of them. The mechanics were hanged. Fifteen men, from a wire strung diagonally across the tunnel, and all of the personnel were forced to watch—not just the deportees but the civilians, too, the clerks and typists, who screamed as they watched fifteen Russians being hanged underground by the light of incandescent bulbs, while guards stood around with machine guns at the ready. "One of the women found the courage to bring me some bread in the barracks the other day," Zdravko said. "What did I need with her bread? She couldn't redeem herself with it, much less change anything." We protested that he was wrong to have refused her; she had after all taken a huge risk by entering the underground barracks where Zdravko bandaged the injured. He should appreciate the courage of such an act. Zdravko didn't argue with us. He seemed lost in thought. A siren went off, and the lights went out. In the dark, Zdravko was still silent; all we could hear was the sound of his footsteps on the floor.

That night we could hear the sound of something like a tin-whistle drifting up through the narrow vents along with the drafts from the shafts and tunnels, the lament of hundreds of thousands inside the earth. Stane scraped his wooden shoe across the floor and asked if anyone knew how Mladen was doing in Nordhausen—it had been bombed recently. At that very moment Mladen walked in. We were astonished. He was pale and drawn. "What's wrong with you, brother?" we asked. He was unable to sit; Stane supported him with an arm around his shoulders. "You're lucky," Mladen mumbled. "This is heaven. In Nordhausen the infirmary's in the factory, big, fat pipes running over the bunks. The Kapo's a pederast and hits everything that moves. Even the medics have to watch out." Then his head fell as if his neck were broken. We all stood by, concerned and unsure, as he whispered that it was his guts, that he had typhus. "No, no, what typhus," Stane assured him paternally, but Mladen said nothing. He said nothing later, as he lay in a room with a multitude of patients, and where I also slept those few days. A Polish doctor set his stethoscope over Mladen's left side. He said there was a problem. Mladen agreed. A second later he cried out that planes were coming and waved his arms. "The wall's collapsing, can't you see?" he shouted. "If pneumonia sets in, he's finished," the doctor said when we were out in the corridor. From then on we approached Mladen's bunk like shadows, and like shadows we withdrew. He lay on his back, his face looking thinner because of the white shirt he had on, the ridge of his small nose more conspicuous. His features were focused, as in Dachau. It was said that he had been a musician, which was probably true, because he would listen to you as though he could hear something you couldn't. We stood watch over him, perhaps hoping he would end the trick he had played to get out of Nordhausen. And we were silent, because although we had been dealing with death month after month, our practice had been to exclude ourselves from it. In the same way one removes one's friends and relatives from fires and other catastrophes, bringing them to safety in one's thoughts, depositing them on a weightless, invisible island of shelter. This is why we medics were so dim-witted about the death of another medic. We were no longer observing death from a distance.

One night, Mladen slid out of bed and fumbled his way to the latrine, and returned. I reproached myself for not waking up and covering him, protecting him from the cold. But it was too late. Every medic is familiar with the gurgling in the chest and knows what it means. We weren't sure what to do as we leafed through the notebook that he kept under the sheet at the head of his bunk. Perhaps we hoped to find something that would console him or like a talisman strengthen the guttering light in his eyes. Finally we found a picture of a blonde girl, with a finely penned inscription on the back: "Your Mimica." It was unusual for a deportee to be able to hold on to a notebook, and especially a photograph, and it was nothing less than a miracle that this fair-haired woman suddenly appeared among the doomed bunks—a miracle that would save Mladen's life. At the sight of her beautiful face we forgot about him for a moment, and we turned into a tribe of savages for whom the photograph was a magic charm. "Mladen," Miran whispered, holding the picture up, "here's Mimica, Mladen." Mladen was silent; there was a slight flickering of his closed eyelids, like the last swell of the sea before it becomes still. We realized that the name had reached him. His face calm, he smiled and murmured, "Lake Bled, you know . . . She was there . . ." Stane ran to get some Coramine, but the injection was useless.

Miran and Stane asked the head medic to do an autopsy. Almost as though, still not fully believing that Mladen had died, we hoped to find not the cause of death but some faint spark of life hidden deep in his body. And so we climbed the steep hillside over which the men in black gloves hauled bones from the trucks. We slipped as we climbed, and our hands sought the knobby stumps of the saplings that had been broken on the muddy slope. But the stretcher bearers didn't slip, possibly because of the weight they carried. When we reached the top, we saw nothing at first, only billows of smoke. Then the pyramid appeared, long tongues of flame licking it at the base. The stretcher bearers shook their logs onto the pile, while a figure holding a long candle snuffer repositioned a limb or two hanging out of the heap. We paused for a second to watch the smoke as it caressed skulls and escaped through open mouths. Facing the pyramid, we were witnesses, but we were also a committee accustomed to such scenes, a board of examiners convened to give them some propriety. We conducted ourselves like officials; we were calm, as though Mladen were one of us, not the object of our inquiry.

We entered a log cabin. The first room was like a cramped entryway of a mountain cabin, except for the earthen pots used for the ashes of cremated Germans. It appeared that the Germans no longer enjoyed this time-consuming privilege, for the urns were empty and lined up on the floor against the wall. Mladen lay on a stone table in the next room. A young Frenchman pulled on pink gloves that were missing the tip of the right thumb. A stocky, muscular young fellow, he talked obsessively, like someone trying to divert attention from something. We kept our eyes on Mladen, on his eyes, in order not to see the breach that was being opened in his body, starting below the chin. He was peaceful, as if waiting patiently for the outcome of his operation. Submitting to his fellow medics' stubborn quest, yet aloof, with a hint of weary sarcasm at the corners of his mouth. Although the small triangle—a human heart—opened up like a box under the garrulous man's knife, its mystery was nonetheless preserved. "A defect," the man said, holding the heart in an agile hand

and poking his knife around the valves. I looked at the unpainted stucco on the wall behind the stone table. I could see every single grain in the gray, damp stucco. Mladen's wan face lay before it like the face of a young woman who has delivered a stillborn child, all her labor in vain. The Frenchman set the heart aside and attacked the lungs. With his broad hands he was soon squeezing out thick ink. "Pneumonia," he said. I glanced at Mladen, who looked relieved at feeling no more pain. The head doctor entered the room, a tall Dutchman with scornful eyes. The young Frenchman grew a little less chatty, especially after he made a comment on the liver and the doctor, eyes flaring, said that exactly the opposite was true. The Frenchman began to stutter; he was probably only a medical student who had passed himself off as a coroner in order to save his life. The head doctor knew this and refused to let him blather in his presence. He wanted to be shown the heart and the lungs, but didn't contradict the diagnosis. The medical student stuck the scalpel into the gut, slicing it open lengthwise as a salesman cuts through a piece of cloth with half-opened scissors. He stopped to inspect a spot. "No," the head doctor said. The student continued cutting, stopped again, looked, and said, "Typhus." The head doctor nodded and said, "Typhus." Then he lit a cigarette. To me the pleasure he took in the cigarette seemed irreverent, and yet I was pleased to see him standing so tall and confident in his striped clothing. I was pleased too that he had honored Mladen in this way.

The Frenchman tossed the intestines onto a heap, not bothering to suture the incision as the coroner in Dachau did. I remembered how Mladen had balked at having to watch a dissection after the short medics' training Dr. Arko gave us. "I can't watch," he had said. But you were wrong, I chided him quietly as we left the cabin. You were wrong, Mladen, you should have forced yourself, then perhaps you could have resisted death. I was being childish, and knew it, but I kept repeating to him that he'd been wrong and that he needed to know death, which was what our fathers said when they returned from the Soča front. "You mustn't be afraid of death," they told us, "because if you're afraid, death will come for you." We made our way down the hillside—carefully, I thought, because the whole hill was alive. Any second we could step on a human heart, on Mladen's heart, or on his eyes. Stretcher bearers went past us, carrying more fuel to the top. From one of the stretchers hung a bony arm, dragging on the ground, its haggard fingers trying in vain to clutch the earth and escape the fire.

I have returned to the steps and slowly make my way to the uppermost terrace. These narrow terraces remind me now of the ones around Trieste, which rise steeply from the seacoast to the edge of the Karst's plateau. There they conform to the contours of the hills; they hide beneath the acacias and dense brambles. On either side are vineyards whose old vines challenge the sun and slowly force it to mellow the copper earth's juices in deep-blue bunches of grapes. Back then, I never thought of those magnificent steps that link blue sea and azure sky, or of the trellises that range across the long, dark terraces.

Here death held a harvest that lasted all four seasons, and in each season the juice of our life dried up and ebbed away. Yet as I look at the names carved on the surface of the short, obliquely cut columns, I tell myself that there were places where the devastation was far greater. Buchenwald. Auschwitz. Mauthausen. The testimonies from them are a revelation even for a camp survivor. The steps in the quarry at Mauthausen, for instance. A hundred and eighty-six steps. Nine flights. The zebra-striped bodies had to climb a narrow path running along the quarry's edge to the top of the steps six times a day, carrying heavy stones on their backs, and a Kapo standing guard shoved anyone with too light a load into the rocky abyss. That cliff was called the Parachutists' Wall. But you could also fall down the steps, especially if you were thin enough and the stone heavy. The steps were uneven, some at a slant. The guards would sometimes take a prisoner who had just made it to the top gasping and push him back down the steps; he fell into those behind him, and white stones and striped uniforms went rolling to the bottom. A method of killing which differed only slightly from what was done in this quarry, but the scale and precipitousness of those steps are so overwhelming that even one with considerable camp experience feels weak at the sight.

For a long time now I've been aware that my own experiences were modest compared to what others described in
their memoirs. Bláha, Levi, Rousset, Bruck, Ragot, Pappa-
lettera. And that I wasn't observant enough. I was trapped
in my dark world, a hollow world populated by shadows. I
saw with my eyes, yes, but did not allow those images to
reach my heart. This was not a matter of will; at my first
contact with the reality of the camp my spirit was submerged
in a fog that filtered events, that bled them of their power.
Fear deadened me, but also protected me from the greater
evil of accommodating myself to that reality. And so it never
occurred to me to take an interest in the names of our su-
periors, or to join the circles of the influential, or to partic-
ipate in camp politics. I learned about this only later, when
I read the testimonies of others. Even as an interpreter, and
later as a medic, I remained one of the herd, another cell
in the body of mass fear.

The fear permeated me on my very first day at Dachau,
when we climbed out of the cattle cars and walked into the
shower room. Not because I was soft, four years of war and
army life having shaken me free of the rituals of civilized
life. I was not surprised by the press of naked bodies, or by
the shaving of hair, or by the scarecrows in short, baggy
clothing. One learns from corporals about how abstract is
the value of culture and courtesy. Corporals whose nastiness
derives from stupidity or an inferiority complex. The shrieks
in the shower room spoke of a lust for destruction that I

didn't understand but that my body assimilated once and for all. This is why it would be ridiculous for me to describe how pathetic was the shearing of hair in the underarms and crotch, or how badly the liquid disinfectant they painted on underarms and crotch stung. Disaster was in the air. You breathed it. Day hadn't properly dawned before our shaved, anointed, and washed bodies stood naked in the February snow of Germany.

The fear during those first days—the awareness that people could kill you—was childlike. A scene of killing repeats month after month, and if you don't die, you accept it. You accept not that you will die, but that the situation is such that your death is likely. A realization more devastating for a healthy, pampered body than for an organism that is exhausted and whose tissues have begun to atrophy. Certainly, anyone who had dealt with the Nazis outside a camp did not expect anything good inside one. But the shock on first entering the realm of crematoria was overwhelming, as indeed the economy of destruction required it to be. Naked bodies walking and running through snow, waiting in drafty barracks, running some more through snow. I don't remember now whether I was bewildered or horrified. Or how I felt in my knee-length khaki army breeches, socks, and wooden clogs in front of the barracks where we were kept for what seemed an eternity. I must have been freezing, but those memories pale before the endless hours and days we stood on these terraces, huddling together in the snow like bundles of firewood. Firewood that swayed with the mindless con-solation of rocking. In comparison the cold at Dachau was innocent, amateurish, even though it could have been my last if I hadn't contrived to get a vest, which was too small, but the woolen mesh clung warmly to my torso. Obtained for a pack of Morava cigarettes that I had smuggled through the showers, the shouting and the beating and the threat-ening looks and my own nakedness. The cigarettes plus the handkerchief I wrapped them in. Dani had brought them to jail, and the warden, or whatever he was, had given them to me before I left. She must have rewarded him well for that kindness. Little did she know I would be leaving.

We had no appetite for the reddish noontime slop we would eventually long for with our entire being, and then we were again required to strip in the snow and wait outside the warehouse barracks for our zebra stripes. A poisoned vapor hung beneath the low, cloudy sky. Though I had eaten little for several days, I wasn't hungry. In fact, I felt no hunger all the way to Alsace. When at the station we caught sight of a French sign painted over with German characters, we felt that we were in familiar territory, among a people who hadn't discarded the laws of the heart, for as our long column hobbled down the deserted early-morning street, wooden soles rhythmically striking the large cobblestones, house-wives standing at windows raised handkerchiefs to their eyes. This was the first and last time in our entire camp experience we witnessed anything like this.

Our education took only three weeks. The sturdiest organisms were the first to go; they had a harder time adapting. Watery rations of food and twelve-hour work shifts in the tunnels. Amid constant drafts. And snow outside. But more than anything it was the pace that devastated. The abrupt departures and sudden returns. Pieces of bread hastily swallowed as the shouting drove the herd to assembly. Exhaustion yet fitful sleep broken by the shouts of morning reveille. No more sense of morning or evening, because the frenzied pace mixed beginning and end, darkness and light. The body lost its center of gravity; it had no sense of the vertical when it stood or of the horizontal when it lay stretched out on a mattress. Even when prone, the body hung rather than lay, the legs slipping downward even in sleep. And the heart, constantly on guard and waiting for the shouts that would propel it out of bed, did not rest and lost its energy. Trips to the latrine were rushed. The boards that formed the floor of the abandoned factory, when lifted, revealed a stream. We would go down to the running water, wash and rinse out our mess tins at one end, relieve ourselves at the other. But quickly, because we had to hurry back up to stand at attention in the snow. No, I wasn't at all hungry, and it took no generosity on my part to give my bread ration to the prisoners from the Karst. At that time they still had energy enough—they didn't yet caress the bread with their eyes as they ate it. They felt pity for me, who looked a goner to them. They made the sign of the cross over me. And I

made it over myself, because I was setting off into the unknown when I slid down onto the floor and refused to go
back in the tunnels. The commandant kicked the sprawling,
striped lump, but even that couldn't rouse it from its apathy.
The truck brought me back to the barracks. It carried a body
in a crate, and me on top of the crate. During evening rounds,
Leif gave me a couple of aspirin and yelled at me for running
only a temperature of a hundred. But I *was* sick. The relative
quiet of a barracks full of the hopeless helped me recover.
The Kapo thrashed us with his club only before the roll call.
Otherwise long, peaceful hours in the barracks. Diarrhea
caused the only disruption, requiring twenty trips a day.
Some didn't move from the pot at all. But diarrhea eventually
brought calm, it subsided hunger and made the body more
compliant. When I lay down on the ground here, which is
strewn with gravel now, I had no desires. The ground is the
best place to rest, even in the world of crematoria. But when
I lay down the third time, I thought that would be my last.
I pulled through again, however, like a tenacious old dog.
Afterward the *Weberei* helped with its ludicrous but peaceful
cutting of strips. And the bandage on my left hand, around
the little finger. Which was when I saw my blood. It was
rose-colored, like water mixed with a few drops of raspberry
juice. It had lost its substance. Then came quarantine, and
Jean. Then I started writing case histories and diagnoses for
Leif. Interpreter and secretary to the prison head physician.
This was not an official camp assignment, and I have no

idea under what title I was entered in the infirmary lists—clerk, assistant, orderly? An exception was made for me, as it has been repeatedly throughout my life. I am never weighed on the usual scales. In this instance, it meant escape from chaos into peace and order.

At Leif's side I could help people and be useful, and justify somewhat my separation from the crowd jostling in the barracks. Then, as the camp was being evacuated, Leif said goodbye to me and went with his friends, and I returned with the infirmary to Dachau, and while the doctors and medics retained their positions, I became an ordinary serial number again. In Dachau we had to roll up our sleeves. Outside the showers and inside the showers. Dear old Tomaž, who had been so happy at the prospect of going to Dachau because he would be closer to home, was one of a multitude who turned into a mass of garbage like the rags, fetid bandages, and wooden spoons that were shoveled out through the windows. When I read the accounts of other survivors or think about my own experience, I am struck by the finality of the world of the ovens. In those necropolises it did not matter what department you worked in. Barbers shaved death, quartermasters dressed it, medics undressed it, registrars entered the dates of death after the serial numbers, and in the end they all, each of them, were sucked up the huge chimney.

When we lifted all the bodies still breathing off the mattresses on the parade grounds at Dachau, I had to separate from the infirmary staff and join the crowd in the quarantine block. There I was lost among a churning, shapeless mass. My panic was especially keen at night, when time came to get in the bunks; instead of blankets we had paper sleeping bags, which rustled endlessly before their contents finally settled down. We were packaged merchandise crammed onto shelves that could be emptied at any time, I thought. To ease my anxiety I told myself that a body inside a bag was isolated and therefore independent; that the bags had not been used before and were therefore clean, much cleaner than blankets. Then the rustling that came from a bunk in the corner reminded me of the sound of a field of corn in the wind, and I thought of Uncle Franc's in Mrzlik, and said to myself: cornstalks, cornstalks, cornstalks. As if to hyp-notize myself.

The lethargy of the quarantine block was broken by the aerial bombardments, during which one could see planes being downed; and later by the experience in Munich, where the rubble had to be cleared. I was not sent to Munich. I owe a debt of gratitude for this to the caring hand that assigned me to the medics' corps. Someone knew about me—unless it was a mere coincidence. The inmates would leave well before dawn and return exhausted at night, and just as they were falling asleep they had to start the cycle over again. Only occasionally did they manage to satisfy their hunger. Once a bomb destroyed their convoy and they were left with kettles full of army rations. They took off their striped jackets, tied the sleeves shut at the cuffs, and filled them with the thick stew.

But I was now in the infirmary. In block 15, known as the *Scheissereiblock,* the shit block. What my room later in Harzungen would be in a small way, this block was on a large scale. Four rooms, two hundred diarrhetic patients to a room. A hospital with a stench so miasmic that it was useless to try to exhale through your nostrils; you were suffused through your pores. Gradually all your fibers soaked it up and you were virtually one with the smell. It was only if you spent time outside the block, which was rare because so much work had to be done with people lying in their own dirt, that on returning you were hit again by the vapors from a fetid pit. Maybe I owe it to my peasant nature, who knows, but I never had a problem dealing with pus, feces, and blood. While attending befouled bodies my only wish was for them to be clean and lying in bed again, as though a body put to rights externally would be put to rights internally too. Not unlike the ritual cleaning of hands that a criminal instinctively does. Or the German insistence on strict order, which must in part be an attempt to compensate for some inner disorder.

André and I got along well, and our care for the sick was productive, successful. André was one of those rare physicians who combine professional knowledge with an easy manner, gravity with boyishness. He was also less anxious now that the danger of his being sent to Breslau had passed. They had asked for him there even while we were being evacuated from Natzweiler. He was saved by a shortage of transport vehicles. It was said that in Breslau the death penalty was carried out with an ax, and that the executioner appeared in full parade dress, wearing white gloves. But the two fronts were converging, and André hoped that he had been forgotten. He devoted himself to his patients, and I was his loyal medic.

Our good working relationship galled our block Kapo. Josef Becker, a Volksdeutscher—an ethnic German—from Poland. A bastard who had dismissed eighty patients at one toss. André insisted that Becker address him formally, and used the latitude he had as a doctor to challenge him. It was easier for Becker to take his spite out on me, but he came up against my Karst stubbornness. The day he found a paralyzed patient covered with excrement—I was in the middle of another task and had decided to finish it first—Becker threw a fit. Tall, thin, with a narrow, grim face, he was like an unsheathed razor. "I don't like touching fouled bodies," he hissed and ordered me to tend to it right away. I did, but I took my time. I rinsed the skin painstakingly, as though this were the body of my own grandfather. I was silent. It's a trait I inherited from my mother, that persistent silence. Becker would have liked me to protest, anything so that he could let loose. But I said nothing and thought how pathetic the human race was: here was a man who had dismissed from the infirmary people that couldn't stand straight and had to shove dirt into their rectums to keep from fouling the floor on their way to the latrine, playing the good Samaritan. Obviously I couldn't stay a medic for long around a Kapo like that. "If only you could bend a little," my companions would chide me. They said I could be the room's permanent medic. But I couldn't imagine forcing myself to appease the Beckers of this world. So my name was added to the list of medics to be transferred to Dora. Dr. Arko set up a special course for us; we learned more than most medics, and eventually knew more than some of the self-professed camp physicians and surgeons. Certainly more than the one who tried to remove a tumor from a patient's calf by cutting through the muscle. Dr. Arko arranged for us to attend one of Dr. Bláha's autopsies, so that we would at least get a rough idea of the body's inner structure. That was my first official entrée to the building in front of which I had been depositing the corpses from my room. Those trips took place early, as day broke slowly and sluggishly. The wheelbarrow squeaked, its tin cover grated, but I heard only the silence of the bodies I carted, and the silence within me as I pushed past the rows of barracks.

Ravensbrück. Oranienburg. I was never there. But Belsen I am familiar with. We stayed in the military buildings, never seeing the area where human remains decomposed, though it was close by. The world learned of Anne Frank after the war, but during the war there were a thousand Anne Franks. Our Zora was one of them: Zora Perello, who had the face of a madonna and whom we all adored. But we Slovenes are too negligent a people to have collected Zora's letters or her diaries from the period that preceded her imprisonment by the Germans. For many years before that, she had been a prisoner of the Italians, refusing to accept the thralldom of Slovenes in the Kingdom of Italy. We wouldn't know how to present her to the world. To this day our nation's meager soul has not managed to free itself from the cocoon of its pain. We embrace our warriors, the heroes that fell on the battlefield; after centuries of subjugation they are a miraculous flame rising from the ashes. But it does not occur to us to celebrate the fate of a young girl, a beautiful high-school student. Like all small people we have a penchant for the gigantic. After the war, when I returned to Trieste and learned that Zora had been at Belsen at the same time as I was, the same desolate feeling came over me as when I watched the Alsatian girls led from the bunker to the barracks with the chimney. If Zora's wasted being had come under my care, I may have been able to preserve the pulse of life in her body, however weak it was. I may have been able to help her in some spiritual way, my presence alone keeping the dim light in her eyes. The daydream of a young man denying the irrefutable evidence of his helplessness. Or was my disconsolateness so intense because this was a female life that had been lost?

We were now waiting for the liberation. We had ears only for the thunder that approached like a giant steamroller on hollow earth. When the rumbling subsided, a limitless, in-comprehensible stillness took over. The stillness that made the cry of the zebra-striped crowds that greeted the moment of salvation all the more wild. It was the voice of hunger and of joy, of stark terror and indiscriminate thanksgiving, the yelp of an inarticulate animal and the howl of a human being still fighting for mastery over the animal in him. In the midst of this excitement, my lungs started acting up again. It was evening. I was walking along a sandy path back to the infirmary, and as I walked I left red drops behind me like a wounded but tenacious animal. We were waiting to be evacuated, and for me to give up the ghost with the first breath of free air would have been cruel. I don't know how I reacted to the blood, I can't remember anymore. Maybe I started running. Maybe I just kept walking, pressing a rag to my mouth, as I did in the washroom at Harzungen. I was worn out, and as we were being transported toward the Dutch border, I half sat, half lay against the side of a British truck.

Belsen! Too big a name for such a small strip of earth. The fate of a single room in one barracks there was equivalent to the fate of twenty or thirty here in Natzweiler. The bar-racks on this terrace were full of convalescents—a throng of prisoners who lay about and milled around, collected infor-mation, explained, interpreted, and discussed, but above all waited for meals. Waited the endless hours from dawn to midday ladle, from midday ladle to evening bread. Toward nightfall the stomach's demands abated. Darkness veiled the pangs, and sleep dulled them. Dulled them only to your consciousness, of course, because even when half-comatose, the organism kept fighting for the substance it lacked. Because of the large number of people in such close quarters and because of the craving that the square of bread and blob of margarine aroused, darkness loosened tongues and gestures. Our cells began to taste the forgotten pleasure of eating, but that pleasure was just as quickly removed, leaving them anxious and greedy like a nestful of fledglings with beaks open. Just before lights went out there would be talk of menus, feverish exchanges of quarters, halves, whole pieces of bread for tobacco, and spoken or wordless settlings of accounts.

One night I saw a group of prisoners jostling against the wooden wall between two bunks, the jostling accompanied by the stomping of bare feet against the floorboards and by muffled breathing. It was a united effort. A German Kapo who had thrashed so many of them in the course of the day lay on the floor. It was a swift sentence that involved no personal rage. A form of execution that was collective and mindless. But no good comes of witnessing a scene like that. It's not a question of whether the person deserved being squashed like a bedbug; I would have let him expire on his own. Except that these scum occupied mattresses, and thus prevented some ravaged prisoners from recuperating on them, or at least dying in peace. Sometimes, when a Kapo couldn't stay in the infirmary for lack of a mattress, the medics would resort to an injection. That was a procedure the SS itself had introduced. An injection of ether or benzine straight into the heart. Or if neither was available, a shot of air into a vein, causing an embolism. In this way bodies that would have taken weeks more to wither would be lying on the concrete washroom floor the next morning, and the mattresses would be turned over to the condemned henchmen's victims. For the most part, the henchmen were ordinary German criminals, the next-highest authority in the camp after the SS. But there were other nationalities, too. One evening a Polish Kapo, whose job had been to hang condemned prisoners, was put on trial. A Belgian and several Poles questioned him, with Franc interpreting. The defendant said he had done it for the extra ration. He said he hadn't actually hanged the prisoners, they had kicked the stool out from under themselves. There was no time for a long hearing, so the prosecutors clubbed him. As chance would have it, an SS man came into the barracks then, looking for someone, and asked what was wrong with the rumpled heap on the floor. The Pole was so broken that he could not speak, and the prisoners explained that the man had fallen from an upper bunk. The danger passed, but the Kapo didn't survive the night.

Franc has many stories to tell about life in the darkness of the long house. About the Italian who on his sleeve wore a patch with three yellow dots on a field of black, like a blind man, though he could see perfectly well. He sat in front of the barracks, knitting woolen socks. Or about the emaciated Russian who stiffened one day, leaving a French assistant convinced that he had died, and who revived after they laid him out on the concrete. Franc himself experienced something similar. He was helping to carry a corpse to the storage room beneath the oven, taking the ankles while his Russian assistant clamped the long tongs around the neck. They had to heave the body onto the pile there. Then, because of the added weight, the air in one of the corpses on the heap shifted and escaped through its open mouth, like a sigh. *"Chort!"* the Russian gasped, and both of them ran. One day, Franc pilfered a tuxedo from the clothing storehouse. Who could have been transported to this lost world in such clothes? Franc put it on and walked out onto the highest terrace, in front of the mess hall. He paraded through the doomed air, grinning, waving his arms, and waiting for the center of the universe to fly apart. An SS came up behind him unexpectedly, gave him a kick, and shoved him along. Franc was lucky that it didn't go beyond that. When he tells the story, he laughs nervously, sitting on the divan in his small parlor overlooking the Ljubljanica River. "I saw a Resnais movie in which a prisoner is shown dressed in a tuxedo," he says. "The audience thinks it was made up. But I knew better. Of course our setting with its death terraces was not in the movie. It makes a big difference." He's right. The barren, white gravel-covered ground says nothing now. Resnais did manage to create a world which spoke to me, but his *Nacht und Nebel,* as worthy as it is, is still meager. He would have had to immerse himself in the life, or rather, the death of the camp. He would have had to live it. To live the death. But would he have been able to look at it then with a cinematic eye?

Man is capable of anything. He has drunk wine from the skulls of the vanquished; he has shrunk heads. Twentieth-century Europeans used such heads as desk decorations, heads with grinning teeth. Flayed human skins hung in Dachau, Dr. Bláha writes, like laundry set out to dry. They were used to make thin leather for riding breeches, briefcases, slippers, book bindings. This is why it wasn't healthy to have healthy skin, he writes. I may be more or less at home in the reality of the camps, but in the light of some of Dr. Bláha's testimony I am a novice. I never delved into the mysteries of the camp, avoiding them like an invisible ray that could destroy me. Like a child's fear of the dark, or a child's denial.

Leif could sense this. He didn't like my aloofness, and to bring me out he often asked questions about my country. He was a practical man. He would assemble all the prisoners on this terrace so he could examine them and judge their fitness for work. He sat at an unpainted field table, the long lines of naked bodies defiling past him. He separated into categories, for the work details weeding out the atrophied and infirm. Whoever was able to show evidence of gangrene or serious swelling, or point to traces of diarrhea on the bony fins of his backside, experienced a moment of peace beneath the summer sun. The maimed and crippled enjoyed a glimmer of happiness when they were counted among the rejects. Leif didn't set his stethoscope to their chests, nor did he expect me, his interpreter, to ask them if anything hurt. We had no problems until a senile Istrian tried to make him understand how weak he was. Verbose pleas annoyed Leif Poulson, who had been a chief physician in Oslo and considered this yet another example of Italian sniveling. He looked askance at me as I tried to explain to him that the Croatian Istrians were not of Roman descent. He finally acquiesced. From then on he didn't wait for me to object but would ask right away, "How about this one? What group does he belong to?" To be sure, it was unfair for nationality to influence a doctor's decision, but at least this meant that the Kapos wouldn't drive the human herds out of the barracks indiscriminately and pick people for the work details with punches and kicks. In the summer of 1944, the world of crematoria was changing. You could feel the reality of the second front. Every day before we began work, he dictating anamneses and diagnoses and I transcribing them, Leif stopped by the infirmary Kapo's office to check the positions on the wall map. Tall and white-haired, with a stethoscope around his neck, he wore zebra stripes, this captain of a sunken fleet who still hadn't lost faith in sailing the high human seas.

But I'm wrong, it wasn't on this terrace that Leif sat at his field table, it was on a lower one, the next one down. From here you can see the cross beam of the gallows, while on that day the view didn't reach that far. Rain poured at steady intervals, making it useless for us to press our backs together, because the wet rags would only cling tighter to our skin. At first it appeared to be a day like any other. Outside the *Weberei* a Kapo was berating a naked prisoner, whose emaciated body had stopped anticipating attacks of diarrhea. The man was a lawyer from Ljubljana, sticklike and tall, wearing thick-lensed spectacles. "*Verfluchtes Dreckstück!*" the Kapo cursed, kicking him into the washroom, toward the middle where the big lavatories stood. "*Pass mal, wie er stinkt, der Verfluchte!*" One blow of the Kapo's fist sent the man flying, and his glasses fell onto the cement floor. The whites of his eyes shone helplessly in the dark room. "*Bleib da stehen,*" the tormentor shouted, and the culprit's hands clutched the gray edge of the circular basin that enclosed a pillar with holes at the top. Thin streams shot from them every morning, and we had to stick our shaved heads and bare shoulders in the streams. But nothing came from the holes now. The Kapo grabbed a bucket of icy water and splashed it over the body, its spine shuddering like an exhausted animal struck with a whip. "*So, Mensch.*" Then another bucket. Each douse ran down the man's back and over the ladders of his ribs as though over windows veiled with parchment. Then down between the wooden buttocks, causing liquid shit to run onto the hard gray floor. "*So, Mensch, so stinkst du nicht mehr.*" This was an ordinary episode. Anyone could be subjected to that kind of washing.

We dreaded midday roll call, because that was when heavy, sooty clouds would creep across the mountainside and it would begin to drizzle. Then, as we stood in formation on the terraces, rain would come down like water from a fire hose. The Kapo would move from row to row, squinting as he tried to determine whether each row was perfectly aligned. He would kick any offending shin that disrupted the formation, or shove his elbow into a back not straight—all before an SS man arrived to count the barracks dwellers. Then the Kapo, big and powerful, stiffened like a tree trunk and shouted, "*Mützen ab!*" Long rows of hands clutching wet, round caps slapped against wet pants. Heavy gusts of rain washed over the long rows of skulls as an SS man in a brown raincoat, clipboard in hand, counted them, and the Kapo stood holding his cap against his trousers, his chest thrust out, like a gorilla taught to stand up straight. We stood, and our minds strained to drive away the image of the oven, and our hearts prayed for a miraculous return to the world of human beings. And I prayed too, a rhythmic, silent recitation of pleas like the beads of a rosary, like the drops of warmth hidden beneath the arches of my soaked ribs. It was a sincere prayer, born of fear without limits. When the gorilla shouted again, all hands fixed the soaked caps back onto skulls, all bodies twisted in an involuntary attempt to escape the torrent. And on every terrace, all the way to the top, eyes stared upward, hoping that the rows above them would start moving, each toward its own barracks, and that kettles would be brought out from the mess and down the steps. The sight of white steam rising from the watery but hot kohlrabi made every capillary go wild with longing, every pupil dilate with greed. You feel that the emptiness inside you is about to swallow your last shred of reason. The rows above refuse to move. The hovering cupola of sky presses its darkness tighter to the hillside. Maybe someone is missing and we will have to wait in the downpour while they search for him, then wait some more while they drag him half-dead to the bunker. The SS man starts up the steps. His boots move quickly from step to step while rows of eyes follow the fluttering of his waterproof coat through the veil of rain. Maybe he's just now checked the bunker and crematorium, and they'll tell us we're dismissed when he reaches the top. But the rows on the terrace above are still standing in place, and the ones above them. Only a muffled whispering stirs our formation; perhaps it isn't even whispering but only the sound of wet rags rubbing against each other. The storm abates. Along with the few raindrops that the wind carries through the air comes the dull sound of a wooden mallet from the topmost terrace. It seems to be striking a heavy beam. The somber sky is slowly dissolving. Why the mallet blows? The mind races in terror, eyes dart right and left and finally settle on the backs of the prisoners on the next terrace up. These backs are uncertain, too, straining forward, anxious, because the view is just as obstructed by a row of backs on the next terrace. Someone says something. The Russian? Really? At that moment the backs on the next terrace straighten, as though the SS man has come back to recount the rows. In the air the feathers of a black bird of prey gather, and the bird pecks at the mountaintop's wooden skull. Mallet blows again. The rows begin to move. At first on the highest terrace, then lower and lower. Slowly. The heads all turn to the right, toward the top steps of our forsaken pyramid, where a young body hangs, as if from a ribbon of spittle that the bird secreted from its beak as it beat the dark clouds with its wings. The body swings as the kettles are brought out from the kitchen. Instinctively the rows pick up speed the closer they come to the barracks, breaking into a run just outside the doors. They feverishly grab their mess tins, jostling each other as they sit down at the tables. The ladle dips into the kettle. For eighteen hours the kettle has been at the center of our thoughts. At last we can put our faces over the bowls and swallow the hot kohlrabi. Our wooden spoons hopefully seek a few potato peels, scraping the iron bottom of the bowls.

I am standing before the gallows now, its wooden beak jutting greedily into the summer sky. At its base is a square box whose lid lowers diagonally when you press a pedal with your foot. The pedal is in the back, behind the post. If you press it slowly, the victim's feet slide across the surface of the lid and the noose tightens around the neck. Now I understand why we stood here so long. It was a new means of prolonging death. The Germans seem to require a slow rhythm for their sadism. Perhaps this morbid insanity derives from some perverted sex drive, certainly evident in the zeal with which the regime sterilized and castrated. During the experiments to lower body temperature in ice water, Himmler insisted on having the frozen bodies of male inmates resuscitated with the warm bodies of female inmates. He even came to Dachau himself as an observer and was greatly amused to see the female warmth arouse whichever males had not died in the experiment.

The crude, wooden gallows is the spitting image of the one on the Piave where during World War I Czech patriots captured together with the Italian soldiers were hanged. I'm thinking of the photographs in Matičič's book *On Bloodstained Fields.* The rows of gallows that General Wurm put up the length of the front from the Piave to the Tyrol for more than a hundred legionnaires. I can see the boots of the hanged men almost touching the ground and bystanders gaping in a semicircle. Anyone can come and watch. A spectacle for the public's edification. There is another picture in Matičič's book that shows an executioner adjusting the noose around a Czech man's neck. The Czech's hands are tied behind his back, and he stands on a crate beneath a tree into which two pieces of wood have been driven to form a triangle. The body is peaceful, the expression of the face bitter yet absent. The eyes are closed so the mind can be alone. Maybe the man has returned home briefly to bid farewell to his native forests, to his wife. But his features have already parted with all of that. They show a quiet and concentrated masculine sorrow, a defiant solitude. He could never have imagined that his love of freedom would end in an Italian garden, rapacious hands zealously busying themselves with his neck. His face is a curtain that has fallen on everything human. He is not even aware of the soldier who leans with his right arm on the tree trunk, eyes on the crate where the victim stands, impatient for the moment when he will be able to kick it out from under him.

The young man who was hanged here during noon mess laughed in the faces of the assembled camp brass. When they untied him after the first attempt failed, he was so in control of himself that he spat at the representatives of the new European order. Anne Frank wrote that in spite of everything she never lost her faith in fundamental human kindness. That's fine, but the question is: When will the human race be organized—and who will organize it?—so that kindness and not cruelty can be realized?

The tour guide has brought his group up here. Leaning on his cane, he explains to them the technique of slow strangulation. I move away, toward the center of the terrace, where I see a stretch of narrow-gauge rails, an overturned cart, and a pile of granite stones. Simple, solitary objects, more eloquent than all the long disquisitions about starved bodies struggling with granite in the quarries. I never experienced it, but I am sure that if I had been required to haul those huge cut stones, I wouldn't be standing here today looking at this display. The proximity of the tourists agitates me. It's as though I didn't arrive this morning from the outside world but was waiting for them here, greedy like all prisoners for any scrap of news, any shred of life that they have brought with them. I join them again and listen to the guide. He tells the story of a Czech who was a professional gymnast, a champion in the pole vault. Somewhere the man had got his hands on a long pole, and from the bottom terrace he managed to clear the electrified barbed wire and land in the trees on the other side. Of course he was caught. A murmur rises from the tourists, and I can't hear the end of the story. There are only two possibilities: either the Czech sprained an ankle when he landed and couldn't get away, or he landed safely and ran, but the German shepherds caught him. I move in closer. The guide describes how they brought the Czech before the camp commandant, who was impressed by the boy's skill and told him that if he could clear the fence one more time, he would go free. Obviously the boy was skeptical, but he had no choice but to try again. He took the pole and cleared the high electrified fence without so much as grazing it. But that did not save him from the noose. That was how the German commander kept his word, the guide observes, looking old and naïve propped up on his cane.

I think of the Czech academician in Matičič's book. He had been captured on the Piave. Under the gallows he spoke about freedom and the end of Stepmother Austria, then he proudly refused any help and put the noose on himself. The rope broke. A brave Czech legionnaire jumped up and said that by Austrian law a condemned man was free if the rope broke. The reply, however, was brief: "*Noch einmal aufhängen.*" The academician refused help again, this time saying, "Damn you, have you no shame?" A quarter of a century passed between that "damn you" and the moment when the young Russian spat at an SS commandant here, but the essential qualities of the players had not changed. Slavic pride, Germanic ruthlessness. Indeed, except for love, which indisputably holds first place, high-minded resistance to injustice is the most we can contribute to the salvation of human dignity. To rise above our wretched reality is the great legacy that we pass from one generation to the next, and it has become so much a part of us that no force can uproot it. What a marvelous image, that gymnast soaring over the fence; and I heard the story today for the first time. So somebody did after all try to break the vicious circle of powerlessness and death. The woods beyond the oven did beckon to someone. An athlete and his jump to freedom.

A healthy human being has no trouble making confident pronouncements about how he will act; but when he changes physiologically and mentally, all pronouncements lose their

154

validity. The fluids in his tissues evaporate or drain away, his reflexes diminish, his mind slowly slips into a fog. He needs that fog because he is constantly in the presence of death; it keeps him from going mad. When one becomes a shadow, all his movements are slowed down and drawn out. Then mass resistance is the only possible salvation, for it allows all the remaining sparks of energy to unite in a fire. The few attempts I know of—such as at Mauthausen—were mass attempts. A whole barracks would rush into the night and throw their mattresses over the electrified fence. Certainly, very few got past the machine guns and the dogs, but each one of those who fell saved his humanity.

I should head toward the exit now, but I put it off as I did earlier when I couldn't bring myself to climb back up the steps. I look around at the sloping hill and already feel some of the nostalgia that will engulf me once I am outside again. Now I am in the noiseless cemetery of which I was once a resident, which I left temporarily, and to which I have returned. I am an inhabitant of this place. I have nothing in common with the people who are now approaching the door strung with barbed wire, and who will soon be itemizing their experiences, dividing up their hours and minutes. This is the outpost of a perished land that extends into infinity, never intersecting with the human world. There are no points of contact between them. I am attached to this land the way some people are attached to the Sahara, where one becomes mere flame among fire, so permeated by its emptiness and limitlessness that away from it he feels incomplete and longs to be reunited with it. Except that the desert's fire is clean, its sand innocent. Here human hands stoked the ovens; here the soil is mixed with human ashes.

Here there is no interruption in space as in other camps; nothing blocks the view or extends out of sight. Everything is visible, set out logically. Yet I miss something, I don't know what it is. I'll leave with the rest through the wooden, wire-wrapped door, taking some of the air with me into my fragmented everyday life. Maybe I need to take something besides the air and the silence. Something that wouldn't erase the images but destroy their dreamlike power. Except there is nothing to take. Finally even this visit, which has added a scrap of meaning to the aimlessness of my days, turns against my will into a pious gesture. But let it. Let it be a tribute to my perished companions. There is nothing living here for me to take back. No revelation. Or rather, only the revelation that there is no deity that can be both omnipresent and mute before this chimney. Before the gas chambers. No, if a deity does exist, it must be inherent—in the earth, the sea, and man—and unable to distinguish between good and evil. All of which once again suggests that only man can shape the world in which he lives, only he can change it into a place more bearable, at least by his own measure. Then we could approach the ideal of goodness we have dreamed of since time immemorial. But now I have to leave; there is nothing I can take with me from this magic circle of rusted barbed wire.

I am outside, standing in front of the monument that rises forty-five meters above long, thickly sown rows of white crosses. Each Frenchman turned to ashes in this world of German crematoria has his own cross. *Nécropole nationale du Struthof,* a national graveyard. The monument is truly impressive, a sign of the love of a great country for its sons and daughters. The left half of the column is carved into an oblique, sharply falling serpentine that winds inward at the base. Emptiness has siphoned off the right half, leaving only a sharp, vertical edge. Inside this powerful symbol of life cut short the sculptor put the figure of a rachitic body helplessly trapped in white stone. Trapped in the merciless grip of a stone quarry. At the very top of the monument is a sharp, triangular spearpoint that punctures the sky, while the figure is turned toward Donon, the entire vast amphitheater of the Vosges sprawling before its vacant eyesockets. How appropriate to have a national cemetery here, in a space still surrounded by barbed wire, as by a net protecting it against the club of human forgetfulness. Because we so quickly shunned the returnees from the death camps and so quickly forgot those who didn't return. Almost as if it was decided that the humiliation these people experienced in camp should accompany them through life, that that humiliation should be branded on their foreheads like the tattooed numbers our women have on their left forearms in memory of Auschwitz. Why should that be? Why the halo of heroism for those who fell with rifle in hand, while for those hollowed by starvation only a hastily spoken acknowledgment followed by silence? Why is the uninvited guest shaken off so treacherously? Were the prisoners who worked behind enemy lines any less heroic than the armed insurgents? Weren't they in fact more heroic? For if they were caught, they could rely only on their strength of spirit, while the heroes wreathed in glory had weapons to defend themselves. Why this double standard? If a few misbehaved or even collaborated with our oppressors, why should this shadow of shame fall on the great multitude of corpses and the lesser multitude of survivors? But we are at fault—we the survivors—because we never objected. Disillusioned by the postwar world, we withdrew into ourselves, we quietly retreated to regions where only weeds grow out of the injured earth. Instead we should speak out, not only for the sake of our incinerated comrades but to remind the world of the value of a sacrifice which even more than sacrifice in battle belongs in the records of human honor.

I walk along a path that leads from the camp up to the quarry, but I'm not headed there. To the left is forest; to the right, by turns, pastures and rocky slopes. Now and then a car appears around a bend, and the passengers' eyes catch on the pedestrian who in the gathering darkness is about to merge with the mountain. Curious, that lone wayfarer, for they can tell by his gait that he has no destination, that it is a matter of complete indifference to him which way he turns. I get the same looks when I walk down the road to Duta, and then I usually turn off into the park beside the schoolhouse. Today I probably strike the motorists as the shadow of a corpse who in his wanderings through vast fields of timelessness has inadvertently stumbled onto a major thoroughfare. For a second the driver isn't sure whether he should slow down or speed up. Maybe my walks are pointless, but I believe that sooner or later human beings will grow tired of the frenzied cities, the feverish scuttling through their labyrinths, with wide-open green and red eyes everywhere. I believe a time will come when human beings will disband in search of greenery, forests, and rivers, and take stock in silence of all their past delusions. Not that they will repudiate civilization; but they will finally understand that urban conglomeration is no salvation. They will regroup and begin listening again to the earth. Assuming, that is, we don't first obliterate ourselves with the atom. That is the unknown in the equation.

When I was here the year before last, I didn't think about such things. My walk down this desolate road was anxious. Then, as today, I had climbed the old steps and stopped on each terrace. That was merely movement through familiar territory, passage through an intimate atmosphere. But the minute I found myself standing at the edge of the somber woods, an electric shock ran through me. It was as if untrammeled nature had suddenly jolted me awake. As if despite all the long months I spent here, and despite the years of memories, I had only now discovered the evil shapes within this mountain. The hillside I had just left behind, I realized how carved up it was. A leaden darkness upon its desecrated slope, soundlessly splitting all its layers, and a chill from the opened abyss engulfing the entire mountain. As if the earth had been rent and inside it dark fetuses like bundles of aborted children were beginning to awaken. But there is no way I can express what I felt then. All the corpses were present for me on this road sheltered by a high black ridge of trees, but they were not ghosts moving among the thick and quiet shadows but a throng in close formation, defending its territory from the curiosity of a neatly dressed citizen out for a summer stroll. This time I have no such feeling. I think of the long columns setting out for the quarry, and I am reminded of the sudden and horrid foreboding I had two years ago that I would run into a zebra-striped column as it hobbled around a bend in the road. Could I possibly have been afraid of meeting those who are always with me and I with them? No, I would prefer to think that in the silence of that night I experienced a rare insight, the kind artists and ascetics occasionally enjoy, an awakening from the torpor into which death had cast us. For here, outside the barbed wire, the mass destruction had fused for me with the limitless solitude of nature and the universe. It was a direct contact with naked reality, with utter emptiness, with nothingness, with the truth that no human emotion can ennoble.

Struthof. Half a kilometer down the road from the camp toward Schirmeck. A short path branches off from the asphalt and broadens as it meets the mountain inn. Some distant relative of the Mountain Eagle in Trenta. I am here to see the low building to the left. It was erected as a separate bunker, on a gentle incline. The door is wide open, and the white tiles on the walls suggest a country bathhouse. Yet the moment you stand before this white cell you understand that its designer had no love for his fellow man. You shudder at the wave of emptiness that surges from the room and dwarfish building. A real bathhouse retains the blissful memory of warm jets of water and the trace of wet footprints, retains them even when discovered centuries after being buried under Vesuvian ash. Back then I knew nothing definite about this bathhouse. It didn't interest me, or rather I instinctively avoided the thought. Now I know, from material published since the war, that Professor Hirt was consigned eighty male and female prisoners which Joseph Kramer, the camp commandant, got from Auschwitz and gassed amid these white tiles. Professor Hirt preserved the bodies at his anatomical institute in Strasbourg, to enable him to study the somatological peculiarities of subhumans. His special interest was Jewish-Bolshevik commissars. As the Allies approached

Belfort, all the bodies, preserved in 110-proof alcohol, were dismembered and burned. Thus Professor Hirt was unable to make his hominoid plaster casts, nor had he time to remove the soft parts of the bodies in order to retain at least the skeletons. At his trial Joseph Kramer described how the women had to go through this door naked, how he poured Hirt's crystals down the pipe and into the chamber, and how he observed the women through the window. That part of his deposition hangs on the wall to the left of the entrance. The women were gassed in 1943. The following year, when I was here, the chamber was used mostly for Gypsies. I saw them in block 5 when I started as Leif's interpreter.

I don't recall where the SS man seized one group of Istrian Gypsies, from the barracks or from the terrace. In any case, he lined them up in front of the office. Like animals before a storm or an earthquake, they showed an uneasiness unlike the kind that comes from an empty stomach, and unlike, too, the light shiver you feel when selected for a work brigade. History has equipped the Gypsies, more than all other Slovenes, with an ability to distinguish shades on the rich scale of foreboding. They began to squirm and snort like horses when the smell of fire reaches their nostrils. The SS man was an old stableman and abusive: he cursed and struck them on the head. He shouted, "Goddamn Gypsies," and they countered as wise peasants counter an inexperienced agronomist. "We aren't Gypsies," they said and pointed to the capital I drawn with a felt pen in the middle of their red

triangles. *"Italiener and Zigeuner—gleich!"* the SS man bellowed and kicked the thin men back into formation, which
they had broken to show him the initials on their chests.
Then one of the men shouted, *"Wir sind Österreicher!"* The
SS man stood stock-still as though commanded by his officer.
"Was?" he asked slowly and deliberately, making ready to
attack the zebra-striped creatures, who were trying, all at
once, to give evidence of this extraordinary declaration.
They spoke in a German that had become so frayed from
disuse since the end of World War I that the man in boots
was totally confused. He tried to extricate himself from its
tangled skein by using the only means the German soul knows
for subduing its age-old problems: He bellowed. Even so he
eventually went into the office for an interpreter. The boy
from Ljubljana he brought with him had difficulty understanding the Gypsies; he, too, raised his voice at them,
German-style, when they continued to insist they were Aus-
trians. But they reached an understanding, which is how
they came back to our block. They were weak from their
ordeal, their eyes darting from face to face as if seeking an
explanation. But it wasn't until later, when I saw a Gypsy
lying on the cement floor of the washroom in block 5 and
puzzled at the bluish froth coming from his mouth, that I
realized what fate our Istrians had escaped. I never asked
where the gas chamber was. I tended the young Gypsies to
whom the professor had given smaller doses to evaluate the
effectiveness of the new gas. I can still see one of them,

gasping for air like an old asthmatic. Whenever I walked past his bunk, his thin, handsome face would follow me, though he knew I couldn't help. Perhaps he wanted me to experience his fate in all its futility and keep him company on his lonely journey.

At last the campgrounds. I have fought the temptation to spend the night in a building of bricks and mortar and sleep in a proper bed in this village of Schirmeck, which sits so conspicuously at the base of our mountain. I can't imagine what odd desire for contrast or counterpoint lured me to this neatly ordered, well-kept domesticity on the night of my first visit. I remember even considering a stay in the attractive inn not far from the gas chamber. But I instantly realized the monstrosity of such an idea. It made no sense for me to try to play the ordinary tourist for a night and assume the emotions to match. Two years ago, here in Schirmeck, the sight of cyclists racing through the village helped me in this respect. I don't know if this road is part of the Tour de France, or whether that was merely a local bicycle race. People crowded the sidewalks, waiting for the cyclists as if this were the Second Coming. I didn't begrudge them the simple plea-sure they were taking at the foot of a twentieth-century Golgotha. On the contrary, I am all in favor of a happy, cheerful life. But the memory of the bicycle race decided the issue of where I would sleep, and I pulled in among the tents as I did two years before. I parked some distance away from the other cars. There is plenty of space, and I am alone at the edge of the meadow. In the lush grass my sandals are soaked with dew as I put down the right front seat and inflate my air mattress. Over the last few summers I have repeated these duties countless times, putting the back seat down, setting the folding chair in the middle, sliding the swollen, soft mattress past it, spreading the sheets and tucking them under, then covering them with a coarse woolen blanket. I have repeated these evening duties from the Alps to Amsterdam and from Amiens to Tübingen, but only here do they turn into a conscious ritual. By the weak light from under the rearview mirror I prepare my bed in this tight space, acutely jealous of the freedom I have acquired. Here, now, under the terraced slope, every fiber of my body is awake. My nomadic life, I realize, is a legacy of my time in the camps. I am not fleeing from community, though, I am simply reaffirming over and over a man's right to a private place into which society may not poke its nose. As best I could, I gave testimony to the living about those who turned into bones before my eyes. And now let me become a free and independent traveler.

I sit next to the bed I've made. I've heated some milk and spread some butter on a cracker. As I drink the warm Vosges milk, I can see the meadow beneath Krn where we sipped that coastal mountainside's lukewarm juice, imagining that it smelled of crimson vanilla orchids. The juice of our native mountains helping us build our strength for the black future.

We had no way of guessing for what kind of mountain we would have to trade the slopes of Tolmin. Yes, I am thinking of André.

I bought his book at the kiosk outside the camp. I was so surprised to have in hand the testimony of a dear friend that it removed the burden of my return to the lowlands. Beneath André's photograph, which shows him in zebra stripes during the liberation of Dachau, are a cross and the date 1954. You're gone, André, having eluded the silent footsteps of our invisible stalker so very many times. Nine years. The measure of time granted you was short. Not nearly enough for you to revel in the radiance of your native fields or satisfy the greediness of your restless eyes. Why didn't I answer the note you sent, inviting me to Sens? You addressed it to me at the convalescent home in Villiers—a narrow slip of paper, the kind you doctors use to write prescriptions. The paper you had at hand, but I suspect that you used the paper that bore your letterhead as a reminder of your victory over the anonymity of night and fog. That was the title you gave your book, too. *Nacht und Nebel. N. N.* The letters that were drawn on your back in oil paint. As was done to the Norwegians and Dutch at first, and later to the French and Belgians. Two big N's across your shoulderblades, which meant that you couldn't leave the camp, that you were to stay and die within the territory demarcated by barbed wire. You say that those symbolic words were taken from a Wagner opera. *Nacht und Nebel gleich!* And that where a human being had been standing, there was suddenly a pillar of smoke. I don't know; I would have to check. But I do know how much the Germans liked to mix music with monstrousness. The music at Dora. The orchestra on our lifeless terraces. The notes affecting them like a drug, like hashish, producing dreamlike visions at first, then inciting the organism to acts of madness. One would have to look hard to find the source of this dehumanization; mere economic or sociological explanations fall short. Chamberlain's racial theory is no help, either. On the first pages of your book, André, you cite Nietzsche's maxim that whoever does not have the will to cause great suffering will never be great himself. Because any female, any slave knows how to suffer. But the first condition of greatness is not to succumb to despair or to the anxiety of doubt when one deals out suffering and hears cries of pain. Creative spirits have hard hearts, he says, and one must attain bliss through hardness, in order to set one's seal on the ages to come. Indeed, these words are the embryo of the world of crematoria, even if Nietzsche did not have in mind the kind of heroes that Nazism spawned. Bertrand Russell maintained that it never occurred to Nietzsche that his superman could also be a product of fear, for a person who does not fear his neighbor, after all, feels no need to destroy him. There perhaps is the true kernel of the German tribe's mad ecstasy. Elemental fear. The elite's fear of missing its one historical chance. And for the masses, fear of the elite, a fear that quickly mutated into adoration of the elite, adoration of irreproachable order and mechanical discipline. Irrationality (Alfred Rosenberg) can also be understood as a product of fear. And there is no doubt that Western capital's struggle for spheres of influence and colonial possessions played a major role. That's why you are wrong, André, when you ask the reader in your introduction whether we shouldn't eradicate the tribe that gave us Nietzsche, Hitler, Himmler, and the million executors of their whims and commands. Without realizing it, you embrace the evil that attacked you. In your holy rage you are no physician. Admittedly, a surgeon attempts to remove the cancer to prevent a metastasis. In speaking of human society, though, we have to be very careful with our similes and analogies. The environment must be changed. It does not help to kill the murderer that the environment produced. The great disappointment for the survivors is not that the German nation has not been eradicated but that the old delusions are allowed to live on for strategic reasons, that comic-opera trials were staged as a public, legalistic mockery of ten million incinerated Europeans. For, as Dr. Mitscherlich observed, not one of the accused ever said in his defense, "I am sorry." I have no doubt, André, that that must have shaken you completely, you who absorbed the stench of decay, pus, and dysentery that we worked and slept in. Yes, you say no mercy for the tribe that poisoned and befouled Europe and the world. I understand you, but you are wrong. And you are gone. André Ragot, a physician from Sens. But for me you will always be a young man in wooden clogs and striped prison clothes, looking boyish with your collar unbuttoned. A self-sacrificing doctor with no fear of typhus. A passionate Frenchman who loves his country and the idea of freedom of the spirit. You, part of our secret, are closer to me than those who are close to me now.

I switched off the light under the rearview mirror and am about to turn in, but for a moment I want to look around. Darkness has erased all the tents, except for one, which sports a broad band of light. It reminds me of a bushy fox tail that my left headlight once caught on the road to Štanjel. In the tent closest to me five or six people sit on folding chairs around a low table. They speak softly; I can't tell what nationality they are. But what does it matter whether they are Norwegian or Dutch. Maybe they have come to this corner of Europe to enjoy nature, to listen to its secrets in silence. But maybe they also know the secret of the two initials, N. N. Maybe they have visited the terraces above, and tonight awful images will populate their dreams.

It probably was no dream, only the impressions from yesterday's visit entangled with the shadows of the Markirch night, that besieged me before I fell asleep. I slept well enough, not waking up the way I did in the campgrounds at Tübingen every time I tossed and turned on my narrow bed. I see myself hidden in a barracks in the evening, waiting for the watchman to lock the outer door to the abandoned cattle pen. He has no reason to think that anyone would want to spend the night in this soundless preserve. He is not, after all, a guard in the Louvre, with priceless canvases to protect. There are no paintings here that would make anybody's mouth water. I step out of the barracks and stand on the terrace. To my right, darkness and the beak of the gallows; beneath me, striped figures huddled on the narrow strips of level ground all the way down the hillside. The barracks are gone, so there are empty spaces to the sides, yet the rows of figures press as close together as ever to keep warm. They are motionless—shadows in burlap, which hangs from their shoulders as from the prongs of a wooden rake. No one was designated to inspect these rows on the terraces. Only I am there. I know that it is not on my account that they are made to stand there against their will, yet even so I begin to feel guilt. Before I have time to consider the implications of this, Leif appears before me at a long table. Now I see lines of bodies standing naked in the sun, waiting to be examined. A crucial selection. But I was only an interpreter at those selections, I had nothing to do with the final decision. I hurt no one. Ultimately, even Leif's choices depended on the most cursory visual impression—the numbers simply didn't allow for any other method. Then why this icy silence from the formations of prisoners? No, they are not assembled here to judge me. Every night, after the terraces have been cleared of living visitors, they gather to resanctify the ground over which so much summer footwear has walked.

They stand silent like orphaned Byzantine saints, gazing defiantly ahead. But someone could at least nod in my direction, acknowledge me. Even if it is a glassy stare of condemnation. Anything would be better than this cold neglect. What is it you think I did wrong? Why do you let me walk past you down the steps like a stranger? Even you, who came from the same block as I? We used to sit together, lie together on the dirt outside the barracks. We pressed our limbs to the earth in hopes that some healing radiation would come from the strata of heavy rock and penetrate our atrophied tissues. Or was mingling with the earth simply an expression of submission, of our desire for final rest, for the silencing of all contradictions and all voices? Our motionlessness was like the waiting of old men, their veins dry, their muscles withered. Except that old men are not so utterly hollow. And yet, on the narrow strip in front of the barracks, we were alert inside, because hunger, until it reaches a certain stage, does not exhaust or mortify; it forces the body into irrational motion, agitated rambling. The greed of the digestive cells is transferred to the ears and eyes, which are on constant, irritated guard to intercept the slightest encouraging noise or reflection. Of course, we knew all too well that no change would come, no surprise, but apparently this alertness itself fulfills some need of the frustrated organism. Take the negotiations over an exchange of bread and cigarettes. All eyes are on a piece of bread the size of a postcard and two fingers thick. It looks like a quarter of an old roofing tile, desiccated and cracked and worn at the edges, because the owner kept it under his shirt to make sure no one stole it at night. The eyes cannot believe that he would relinquish it for a dozen cigarettes; but they do not know the passion of the smoker, the trembling fingers, the working Adam's apple, the rising saliva. All eyes follow the new owner as he presses the piece of furrowed tile to his chest and departs through the crowd to savor each future bite in solitude.

I stand on the steps at the level of our block, in the mountain night, and the prisoners keep silent. Why don't they move? Why don't they call out to me? I know why. It's because of the bread I took from them with cigarettes. I confess my sin. It happened only once, because I never had access to cigarettes again. But that doesn't lessen the crime. I told myself that if I didn't get it, the square piece of bread would find its way into someone else's possession. I vacillated between mercy—to simply give him the cigarettes and appease his smoker's passion—and weakness, my mouth tasting the bread in anticipation. I didn't actually eat the bread until night, though the transaction took place as the day was just beginning. My body was recovering from dysentery, and the mucous membranes of my mouth weren't functioning. Bread had just started to have a smell for me again. During my illness it had tasted like clay, and I gave my ration to others. No, I am not pleading extenuating circumstances. I understood the baseness of my act the minute I enjoyed its reward. I felt unspeakably mean and wretched. So is it the bread you have banished me for, you who all stare ahead? Somebody could at least look my way. Those of you at least who used to rummage through the garbage heap for potato peels. Or who fought for the right to scrape the bottom of the kettle after noon rations were ladled out. Listen to me: you all know what I did later, when I worked as an interpreter . . . But it's true, I wasn't hungry when I worked as an interpreter. Being generous when you're not starving is no great achievement. I concede that. On the other hand, you can't help others if you don't conserve your own strength. It doesn't work any other way. I know what you're going to say. That all we medics, and anyone else who worked in the sick blocks, lived off the bread of corpses. When the stretchers carried the corpses to the storehouse, their squares of bread stayed on our table. Yes, we ate them. I know what you're thinking. That the crime wasn't in eating them but in counting on eating them. We knew exactly whose bread would stay. We weren't constantly, unremittingly hungry anymore, we medics, and we would become so involved in our work that at rations time we didn't focus all of our senses on the food. We didn't receive your bread like the faithful at Communion. We didn't contemplate the significance of your sacrifice. And after we stood naked, for what seemed like an eternity, in the cold dark night, and then greedily absorbed the shower's hot streams, we didn't ask what fuel was used to heat the water. We only wanted the warmth to last, and to be allowed to forget for a while the icy mountain air that would soon grip our naked bodies again. Like the tiles on the floor, we had been installed in this system. We ate your bread un-ceremoniously, like gravediggers putting away the dinner they've earned with their work. We grew accustomed. Man grows accustomed to everything. And apathetic. But you are right to judge me for the bread I received in exchange for cigarettes. I hadn't yet acquired the automatic movements of apathy. I could still feel the gnawing of hungry fox teeth in my stomach, and I knew exactly when I was crossing the line into the realm of base instinct. Yes, condemn me for that piece of bread. Because when the smoker's body finally succumbed, it succumbed in part because of the piece of bread I ate. If I had given him the cigarettes and not taken that one piece of bread, I would not have contributed to his death. Yes, I whispered, you are right to keep silent.

I began moving slowly, carefully down the steps, my tread noiseless because I was wearing sandals and not wooden clogs. It occurred to me that the formations along the terraces hadn't ignored me intentionally but that they simply could not see a living being with their weightless eyes. But, then, I shouldn't have been able to see them. I knew I was dream-ing, yet beyond dreaming. As in camp, I slept, knowing that I slept. The next instant, the door to the washroom flew open and a herd of scrubbed and shaven-headed bodies poured out. Some ran toward the steps and began to scurry up, clutching their shirts and trousers, and the night shadows chased each other over their angular faces. The abrupt, resonant sound of clogs echoed off the steps. No one paid attention to me, so I looked elsewhere. I waited for the chimney up above to ignite into a huge red poppy. But the chimney was black, extinguished. You could see it faintly swaying, because at its base a flock of children had grabbed the steel cable that held it in place, and they were tugging with their little hands as if to topple it. Then the washroom door flew open again, and out came bodies whose bones formed horizontal figure-eights in their sides, and who had what looked like three small, shriveled nuts pressed into their crotches. One of the little girls covered her eyes, but the others stared as if they were seeing endless copies of a broken Pinocchio. Then all the children opened their eyes wide, very wide.

André's question whether it might not be proper to eradicate the race that so desecrated the earth, it raises in me new doubts about collective responsibility. To some extent I accept the axiom that each nation has the government and leaders it deserves. Yet it is also true that people are often the unwitting playthings of larger social laws and forces. The established order fogs their perception of reality. The great majority never disentangle themselves from the phantom created by inherited circumstance and unquestioned habit. Anyone who has a stake in keeping the mass of human chrysalises asleep has a variety of simple methods to do this. Old truths—but essential when judging collective guilt. Both

BORIS PAHOR

the individual and the collective are responsible for whatever ill they perpetrate, but one should scrutinize most of all the society that educated both.

André himself is inconsistent. Even as he rages, he recalls how he once saved Franz, the German who was Kapo of the bunker and crematorium. The SS liquidated all such wit-nesses, but because Franz treated the prisoners like human beings, André hid him in the clinic as we were making ready to evacuate. The ploy didn't work during the first stage of evacuation. But André didn't give up. He slipped Franz into another group that was leaving, and by the time the SS remembered to pick him up, he was gone. André's sense of justice was obviously stronger than his need to punish then.

But when all is said and done, Germans with a heart were exceptional. In my fourteen months in the camps I witnessed only one instance. It happened while our train was stopped at an anonymous station next to a military train transporting antiaircraft guns. It was just after we had buried 160 skeletons from the two front cars, and after Janoš's death. The two cars were beginning to fill again, but the number of walking dead was thinning somewhat. Here and there survivors were finding it easier to stand beneath the raw April sky. Some-times there was room for them to hunker down and die squatting, surrounded by palisades of gray-and-blue stripes. The others, their eyes gone wild, would be left standing, wedged tightly into the thicket of bodies. Only the most brutalized stood on corpses, as one stands on kindling. Those with gangrene or other wounds could force their way to the edge of the open doors. We medics had our hands full. Not that the skeletons actually hoped for a new dressing on their wounds, but the mere sight of disinfectant and the yellow ointment we used, and the ritual with strips of paper, stilled their hunger—a hunger that had lasted six days now, six days on top of their months-long fast before this journey. Across from us stood the military train. The station itself was out of sight. The sky was cloudless, but the sun's rays were feeble, defeated, shining on us with an anemic light that served only to emphasize the barrels of the machine guns pointing skyward. I don't remember if it happened after our futile wait in Hamburg between two trains of prisoners in zebra stripes, or before. But as we did each time the train stood for long periods, we medics scattered among the cars. We realized again how right we had been amid the chaos of leaving Harzungen to occupy a closed car and transform it into our emergency room, with all the supplies we were able to grab: bandages, antiseptics, adhesive tape, ointment, Vaseline, basins, forceps, scalpels, and rubber gloves. Plus a bottle of alcohol from the SS infirmary. Mixed with water, the alcohol served as a food substitute for some and also awakened flickers of hope for survival. The doors of the cars were wide open, and at the edge of the doorways sat bitter figures with their trouser legs rolled up to the knees. The legs were yellow, crusty sticks. Here and there a foot hung out that looked like a club of meat. Attending to a skeleton sitting alone at the car's edge, I set my bottle of antiseptic and paper wrappings on the floor beside him. The man was a Frenchman, no longer young, but still with moisture in his eyes, not the glassy stare of a goner. Although rare, there are bodies still stubbornly resistant despite their cachectic limbs, and such cases are likely to make it to the other side of destruction. He had a lesion on his left calf, and his skin, which was coarse and jaundiced everywhere else, was white and smooth as a bald scalp around the sore. That meant the source of infection was deep down, if it makes any sense to speak of depth about tissue so atrophied. "Does it hurt?" I asked, tapping it with a finger. "*Oui,*" he answered and nodded. He was holding his knee with both hands. Good that it hurts, I thought, and reached for my scalpel. As I glanced back in discomfort before proceeding, I noticed that the eyes of a tall, handsome young man were fixed on me as he polished his machine gun. It was not just a look of curiosity. The eyes were full of astonishment that such creatures were still alive. Astonishment—and the quiet confusion of a proud horse that has had carrion set before it. And the eyes held respect too, almost admiration for the zebra-striped medic handling the carrion so calmly and simply, as if he had had years of experience with this kind of impossible work. My first impulse was to cover the dangling leg and hide the misfortune of that car, of the whole endless row of cars, to hide our humiliation from the eyes of that blond German god. To say nothing of the line of skeletons squatting

under the cars, straining. The sight of their bare shins and
the little heaps of striped trousers at their ankles, particularly
of those who couldn't squat but stood bowed underneath the
car, bumping their bare skulls against it. One skeleton slowly
slid past my patient and became more visible. An unlikely
actor, member of an improbable traveling troupe, appearing
on the stage. As he strained to touch the ground with his
feet, his trousers slipped down to his wooden clogs, revealing
an enormous yellow, bony butterfly. At that point I pressed
scalpel to skin, which was hard as leather, and made a deep
incision from top to bottom. The patient convulsively
grabbed at his knees. Let the young man watch, I thought,
and see how friendly we are with death. Then I stopped
thinking about him. I washed the wound, which exuded a
few tears of yellowish resin, stuffed some gauze drenched
with antiseptic inside it, and dressed it with a paper bandage.
Then I took my things back to our car and scrambled into
my corner. It was cold and I had a cough and preferred to
huddle under my blanket in peace. I didn't want to watch
the soldiers outside, who had stopped cleaning their guns
because mess tins of rice had been brought to them. The
whole train is probably staring at them eating, I thought,
while underneath the car bony fingers scraped like the claws
of an ancient creature. Suddenly René said outside the door:
"He says it's for the one who drained the infection. There
are plenty of us who've drained infections!" Finally he called
to me to come out. The blond noncommissioned officer,

who was sitting at the base of a fieldpiece as he ate from his mess tin, looked up and pointed at me with his spoon. I gave him a slight, tired nod, took a small carton, and returned to my corner. It was half full of rice. Ludicrous of the young Siegfried to think he could redeem himself with it. I sat on my blanket and squeezed the warm, pliable carton in my hands. I hadn't been hungry since I'd started coughing, and found the smell of the rice disgusting. I should give it to somebody, I thought, and was sorry to have accepted it in the first place. My blond patron had probably sent it to me not out of respect for the devastated bodies, but for my workmanship. I held the warm, round carton in my hands and tried to imagine how he saw the long row of caryatids underneath the railway cars, relieving themselves, supporting this crumbling world on their skulls, striped mummies whose bandages kept coming undone and who themselves might crumble any minute. And as I tried to divine his thoughts, I felt as if I had some small, live creature in my hands, a young white rabbit, and the warmth that slowly rose from my hand and up my arm seemed familiar. I closed my eyes and with all my strength forced memory to come to my rescue.

The windshield and the windows glint in the sun. I feel I'm inside a glass ball which, in turn, is caught in a silver net of dewdrops. I've been awake for some time, but am in no hurry to get up and drive in the cold. I'm free of any itinerary, and though I'll probably try to look up Arlette today, I know it would be senseless for me to expect us to re-create the idyll we once enjoyed. We've lived far from each other; my tie is more to the good memory of her from the first few months after the war. I also know that tomorrow I'll be part of the life of the Latin Quarter, that I'll roam through Montmartre and once again have faith in the human spirit. But for now I can't bring myself to move. I suspect that when I get up, I'll drive back to the camp, not to go inside, onto the terraces, but only as far as the gate, so I can take one more look at this dead station. I need an open view, on the off chance that in some concentrated, heightened moment a truth will come to me. Though I deny this childish need for magic ritual, I find it at the same time both compelling and disturbing. When I was awakened by the sunlight that suddenly hit the window near my head, I recalled the squirrel from a story I read to my class. The squirrel kept trying to brush away an annoying blade of straw that tickled its face and wouldn't let it sleep. Finally the yellow blade became so annoying that the squirrel angrily struck at it with its claw and woke up, only to find that the straw was actually a ray of sunlight. I watched my pupils react to the story, the way they laughed good-naturedly at the squirrel and its confusion, the boys so little that they were all eyes and always eager for stories like this.

Now I am looking at children again. Through the dewy car windows they appear framed in rainbows and replicated beyond their numbers. They scramble among the tents. Soon they will be playing catch or swatting at shuttlecocks with rackets, hurling them high into the air. At this moment I couldn't say if there is anything I like more about these summer nomad wanderings than the vibrant pulse of campgrounds in the morning or at sunset as growing boys and girls move to the rhythm of a love they just barely sense. I lie motionless on my bed, with no idea of how I will present the people of those dark barracks to these young things. How I will present those humiliated bones, those humiliated ashes. And I have no idea how my ghosts will find the right words to bear witness before the flock of children darting among the tents, or before the girl who ran circles around the cable yesterday, as if on an invisible merry-go-round.